101 WAYS TO WIN
AN ELECTION

7/1

101
WAYS TO WIN
AN ELECTION

DR EDWARD MAXFIELD
&
DR MARK PACK

Biteback Publishing

First published in Great Britain in 2012 by
Biteback Publishing Ltd
Westminster Tower
3 Albert Embankment
London SE1 7SP
Copyright © Dr Edward Maxfield and Dr Mark Pack

ISBN 978-1-84954-312-5

10 9 8 7 6 5 4 3 2 1

A CIP catalogue record for this book is available from the British Library.

Set in Adobe Caslon Pro and Acknowledgement
Cover design by Namkwan Cho

Printed and bound in Great Britain by
CPI Group (UK) Ltd, Croydon CR0 4YY

CONTENTS

ACKNOWLEDGEMENTS

Over the decades in which we have learned how to campaign, we have worked with thousands of volunteers, colleagues and candidates. All of them have in their different ways contributed to our education and the knowledge we have shared in this book. We are very grateful to them all and singling out any individuals is always a hazardous business. However, particular thanks should go to the three Directors of Campaigns for the Liberal Democrats during our various times working for the party: Chris Rennard, Paul Rainger and Hilary Stephenson.

Thanks, too, to Candy Piercy, with whom Mark has three times co-authored the party's *General Election Agents Handbook*, and to Lynne Featherstone MP and Norman Lamb MP, who were both excellent and supportive candidates as we learned our trade and worked to get them elected. Pam and Paul Corney, and Neil Williams also deserve special acknowledgement for their endless hard work as volunteer campaigners and for keeping your authors (just) on the right side of sanity at the most intense moments of key campaigns.

Thank you to Caron Lindsay and Janet Grauberg for invaluable comments on various drafts of the book. Iain Dale, Sam Carter and especially Hollie Teague from Biteback have all been most encouraging and helped make the book far better.

INTRODUCTION

The man who grasps principles can successfully select his own methods. The man who tries methods, ignoring principles, is sure to have trouble.
Ralph Waldo Emerson

There is a legend about election campaigning in a northern English city from several decades back that involves a mattress, a van, a camera and a ruthless willingness to do what it takes to win.

The legend has it that a guerrilla band of community campaigners shipped the battered mattress from neighbourhood to neighbourhood, dumping it on a street corner at night, photographing it in the morning and reporting it to the city council. Newsletters were printed and distributed to local homes. The council was damned for neglecting the area. A campaign was launched demanding a clean-up. Candidates were run and City Hall was taken. The old guard was thrown from power by a committed team that learned how to communicate with voters and how to galvanise them into action.

It does not matter whether the story is true or false. What matters is what it tells us about the ability of skilled campaigners to change the game.

They understood the core theme that runs through this book: if you want to be elected, you need something to say about things people care about (the message), the ability to say it (the team and the resources), to say it frequently and well (communicate), and the leadership to do all this to an excellent level.

This book draws on each of those themes and expands them into a 'how to' guide for winning an election, giving you 101 tips, each with its own self-contained short chapter.

We have both worked as professional campaign staff for the Liberal Democrats in the UK and have also worked as advisors to campaigns in other countries, including Spain, Australia and several in eastern Europe.

We draw extensively on our experiences in winning (and losing) campaigns from our time with the Liberal Democrats. However, this book is not aimed at candidates from one particular party. Indeed, we hope it will be as useful to citizens who decide to run for office without the backing of a political party as it will to those who choose the party route. We have addressed the book to the candidate but it will be as useful to campaign managers and others involved in the campaign too.

We hope you enjoy reading it. We hope you find it a useful guide to what is one of the most noble career choices to make – putting your name in the public frame, ready for ridicule, disaster and derision, but in search of your contribution to making our world a better place to live.

We hope you put the lessons into practice and share them, too. Remember, you do not win elections by voting for yourself. You win by leading a campaign that is about other people.

PART 1

A GOOD MESSAGE

In this section we ask the most basic, and so perhaps the most important question: why are you running for election? We explain why you need to be able to answer that question clearly with an effective message.

CHAPTER 1

WHY HAVE A MESSAGE?

There are those that look at things the way they are, and ask why? I dream of things that never were, and ask why not? Robert Fitzgerald Kennedy

New York Governor Mario Cuomo uttered the famous line that politicians campaign in poetry and govern in prose. We are idealistic enough to believe that there is room for a little poetry in government, too, but the magic of a well-run campaign can have the same uplifting and enlightening impact as the best of poetry. Just as the best poets have a powerful and emotional message they want to give the reader, so the best campaigners want to appeal to voters' minds and to move their emotions. Democracy is about explaining to people why you and your ideas are the best choice.

Again and again in the course of this book you will be reminded that voters lead busy lives, disconnected from government and politics. As a candidate and a campaigner you will only have brief moments to make your point to them and to make an impact. Your message – why someone should vote for you – should be a simple answer to a simple question. It is surprising how often it catches out aspiring politicians.

Shortly before the 2010 general election in Britain, we were involved in running a training event for incumbents facing a tough battle for re-election.

One session was about 'the message' and each Member of Parliament was asked (without any advance warning) that simple question: why should someone vote for you? Some of the answers were rather rough round the edges. One, however, stood out. This MP – even though they were not the first to answer and so had a little longer to think about it than some colleagues – was utterly floored. The only answers they could provide were about themselves: because they wanted to be an MP, because they liked doing it and so on. They lost at the election.

The lesson is a simple one: you need to give voters a reason to vote for you that will be relevant to them. Your answer needs to be about you but appeal to them. 'I want to win' does not work. 'You want me to win' does. Another example: in 2010, the American actor Kelsey Grammer announced he was launching a political career. Asked why, he talked about the need to complete his life and of actors and politicians having the same narcissistic drive. We do not share this rather cynical view of politicians (we cannot comment on actors) but more importantly we cannot help feeling he needed a better message. One that says why anyone else should want him to run rather than one that focuses on himself.

Nevertheless, beware bland platitudes, too. It is no good telling voters that you will simply do the job they expect you to do. Your message needs to capture why you will do a *better* job than the others will. It needs to be brief, credible and real. Brief because voters have better things to do than listen to you. Credible because voters are smart enough to figure out when they are being sold snake oil. Real because you need to believe it too – only then will you be able make your case convincingly.

Voters are not memory magicians. They do not remember everything everyone says, especially on a topic such as politics that most of them spend most of their time paying little attention to. We will talk a lot in this book about the ways you can communicate your message. You will know it is working when people start repeating your own lines back to you without realising they are doing so. Much of that is about repetition but it starts with a message that is clear, powerful and succinct.

It is the bargain at the heart of democracy. Candidates have a duty to persuade and explain. If they are successful at that, they get power.

Once in office candidates must govern and represent well but they will always have to come back to the same basic truth: you need a good answer to that simple question, 'Why should someone vote for you?'

CHAPTER 2

VOTERS GET TO CHOOSE
THE ISSUES

*It's my idea of democracy. The voters get to set
the terms of the elections, not us. They get to decide
what's important, not us.*
Bruno in the TV series *The West Wing*

Follow or lead? This is one of the hardest balancing acts that politicians and candidates in a democracy have to make. It is also one of the areas that is prone to the greatest myth making: politicians who are good at reading the weather often prefer to believe that they are good at making it.

Change requires a movement and movements are driven by belief in a cause. One great skill of a political leader is to satisfy the needs of a broad group of voters and a narrower group of committed supporters. As Wael Ghonim, one of the activists at the centre of the Egyptian uprising in 2011, has pointed out, activists can unintentionally create a gap between themselves and others. Their commitment to the cause leads them to spend more time engaged with the issue. In Ghonim's words, they 'see things others do not see'. As a result, the hyper-activists behind any cause risk becoming disconnected from a wider audience.

The Arab Spring dealt with profound issues and the participants risked arrest, torture and even death.

Comparing this with the banalities of some election campaigns may seem like stretching a point, but the underlying point is a simple one: in a democracy, political leaders must both motivate their activists and also tune their ears to the electorate.

There are three types of politicians who get this wrong: martyrs, missionaries and the misguided. As an example, at its low point in the early 1980s, all three dominated the Labour Party in the UK.

The misguided include most of us at some time or other. A failure to interpret correctly what voters are telling us can lead to election defeat. This mistake is easier to describe than it is to avoid as sometimes the views of voters can appear to be very misleading.

One of the mistakes those 1980s Labour politicians made was to take too literally what voters said they wanted. Opinion polls consistently showed unemployment to be the issue of greatest concern to voters, who then completely failed to respond to Labour's campaigns on the issue. There are probably two reasons for this – firstly voters did not trust Labour to do any better on the issue and secondly the polls masked the point that most swing voters still believed unemployment was something that happened to someone else, not themselves. It was only when Labour faced up to issues of trust and credibility that they started winning again.

Missionaries are so full of campaigning zeal that they fail to see how far their own priorities differ from those of the electorate. The 1980s Labour Party was full of minority interest groups determined to champion their cause but, to be honest, it is a state of mind that appears in any political grouping. Environmental issues often fall into this category, with candidates who believe they are crucial often finding that their obsession runs a long way ahead of the public's, especially in tough economic times. The most successful candidates are able to mix their passions with a more pragmatic sense of more immediate public concerns.

Martyrs are the ones who will doubtless find this book the least useful. They have determined that the electorate itself is wrong. Again, they appear on all sides of the debate and in all parties. Success, though, will not come from trying to sell newspapers that denounce capitalism to shoppers and commuters. If false consciousness and Marxist dialectics are your thing we are willing to admit this book is probably not for you.

Do not get us wrong! We are not such embattled pragmatists that we reject the role of political leadership. Many of the campaigning and communication techniques we talk about in this book can be applied to the task of persuading the public to change its mind. But in the end, in a democracy, it is up to the voters to decide what they care about most. It takes skill and humility to acknowledge this and to campaign in your own voice on the issues that voters care about most. Failure to do so is likely to end in defeat.

As George Eliot put it, 'To the man whose mouth is watering for a peach, it is of no use to offer the largest vegetable marrow.'

CHAPTER 3

HOW VOTERS THINK

Democracy is government by explanation.
Arthur Balfour

A health warning: this chapter uses language also found in books about selling a product in a market place. Some people turn queasy when they see this applied to politics. We know that politics is about much more than selling soap powder but we also know that success in any field can depend on the ability to learn from the broadest possible range of sources.

We are presented with decisions to make coupled with an abundance of information all the time. How do you decide which car to buy? There are thousands of different models available and, when you add in different options on each of them, hundreds of thousands of different choices you could make – without even starting to consider where or who to buy the car from. Therefore, we make use of shortcuts ('heuristics' in the jargon), such as taking advice from family members who are impressed with a particular manufacturer. It is just the same in all sorts of aspects of life, whether deciding within minutes rather than hours to analyse all the different public transport options to get you from A to B or whether deciding who to vote for.

In politics, shortcuts come in three main forms.

First is use of habit and the party label. Just as a consumer may like (or dislike) Apple and use that as a shortcut to decide which portable music player to buy next, without testing numerous different models, so the habit of who you usually vote for or the party that you do or do not like carries a lot of weight. A good candidate should not simply switch party to exploit this! Rather, a good candidate needs to understand the power of those habits and that for many people persuading them to change their vote is like persuading them to change a habit, sometimes even the habit of a lifetime.

Second, and linked to this, emotion plays a powerful role – who do you instinctively like or warm to, and who are you repelled by? Emotions are a very effective shortcut to making decisions, which is why the brain has evolved to use them frequently. This is also one of the reasons why leading politicians find it very hard to shake off their initial media-created image. They might prefer that the electorate engage in a rational analysis of their record, but the reality is voters will use shortcuts to make their decision.

Drew Westen's book *The Political Brain* introduced recent discoveries in brain science to the political world. He argued that you need to sandwich reason between dollops of emotion. That is not to say you should abandon rational stances on policy issues. Rather, communicating what you do and what you believe needs to be framed in the right way – in a way that connects with hearts as well as heads.

A great illustration is the fate of 1988 Democratic candidate for US President, Michael Dukakis. When he was nominated, Dukakis enjoyed a big lead in the polls yet he ended up losing badly. The campaign struggled on a number of fronts but one of the most telling moments was when he was challenged in a TV debate over his opposition to the death penalty: 'If Kitty Dukakis were raped and murdered, would you favour an irrevocable death penalty for the killer?' He gave an emotionless response on an emotion-filled issue. The lack of passion in his answer was deeply damaging, and that mattered far more than his answer. It reinforced the impression that he would make decisions on key issues without understanding how they would affect millions of people's lives.

One of the most important emotions to get right is the third of the main shortcuts. Does someone sound like they understand people like you and are on your side? That is an emotional response, but if the answer is yes – and only if the answer is yes – then that person can persuade you.

That does not mean people will only vote for candidates who look or sound exactly like themselves – that clearly is not the case. What it means is that they are most likely to vote for the candidate who both shares their aspirations and can communicate that clearly in a language that makes sense to the voter.

CHAPTER 4

HOW PEOPLE CHANGE
THEIR MINDS

*It's not enough that we have reason on our side. We
also have to use words and images powerful enough to
persuade others.* Robert Reich

Predicting elections in many countries used to be
easy. The vast majority of people stayed loyal to
one party through their life. It was the party of their
family, their neighbourhood, their class, so swathes of
the country repeatedly returned the representatives
of one party in 'safe seats'. Elections turned on a handful of swing seats and each seat conformed closely to a
'uniform swing' across the country.

Over the last forty years, though, that uniformity
has steadily broken down. Voters are more mobile
in almost every aspect of their lives and that trans-
lates into their voting habits too. So politics is more
fractured and elections more unpredictable. With
more voters open to change, understanding what
makes voters more likely to alter their voting habits
becomes more and more important.

Robert Reich, Bill Clinton's Labor Secretary and a
respected academic, was discussing George Lakoff's
hugely influential book *Don't Think of an Elephant!*
when he made the above comment. In that book,
Lakoff explained how politicians on the left had

developed the habit of making their case only with rational arguments. They tended to ignore the other aspects of persuasion and, as a result, often lost the argument without ever understanding why. Left or right, the lessons are important if you are seeking to persuade voters to back your cause.

Chip and Dan Heath in their book *Switch* came up with an effective analogy to illustrate how people change their minds or switch their behaviour.

Imagine a person riding an elephant along a path (not Lakoff's elephant, a different one). There are three elements to making a successful journey. The rider needs to know what to do and where to go (the rational mind). The elephant needs to be willing to go in the right direction (your habits need to help rather than hinder). The path needs to lead the elephant in the right direction (so that it is easier, rather than harder, to go in the direction you want).

If you want elephant and rider to head off in a different direction, you need to persuade the rider. But she, in turn, needs to steer the elephant, to overcome the inertia of its habits. Moreover, it makes life a lot easier for them both if there is a clear path they can follow.

In little ways we play out these scenarios all the time in our lives. Need to start getting to work earlier? Reset the alarm clock and place it a distance away from your bed so you do not just reach out, hit snooze and end up sleeping to the normal time. In other words, clear the path for your behaviour so it leads you in the right direction even as your instincts kick in during your early morning half-asleep haze.

This might sound somewhat removed from electioneering but think about how it helps you to frame your campaign message. It is a lesson that many environmentalists have learned in debates over green energy, for example. The detailed, rational case complete with scientific references and decimal points only gets you so far in persuading people of the merits of green energy (the rational mind).

However, arguments in favour of it can also be framed using more familiar, less controversial and more widely appealing points about generating jobs and providing independence from unstable dictatorships with fossil fuel reserves. That makes instinctive thoughts such as 'job creation is good' work with, rather than against, the argument (the elephant). Then you make progress easier, for example by calling initially for more choice and better information for the public rather than for wholesale regulatory bans and changes to be introduced tomorrow (the path).

Where possible you need to work with people's habits by framing arguments in terms familiar to them and which work with their instincts. That does not mean accepting that all their instincts are set in stone for all time, regardless of how much you may disagree with some of them. Rather it means that you have to work with the grain to switch people's minds.

CHAPTER 5

SOUND BITES ARE GOOD

A minimum of sound to a maximum of sense.
Mark Twain

We have a secret passion. We like sound bites. In fact, we love sound bites. To campaign successfully you must learn to love them too.

A sound bite is your message in a nutshell. It is a short piece of speech or text, deliberately crafted to capture what you want to say in a way that wins the attention of the audience. Ronald Reagan, a master of political communication, was a master of sound bites: 'Governments don't solve problems, they subsidise them.' Short, clear and with an ideological kick.

It is true that sound bites have had a bad press. Critics say sound bites are too brief for proper discussion of complicated issues.

Ask them to think of the Ten Commandments. Most are so brief you can even put them in a tweet. But each is packed with moral meaning on weighty subjects. Remind them that any good manager or leader knows their priorities – what matters most to fix their firm or their community. That is a sound bite.

You can be brief and be thoughtful. You can be concise and tackle the difficult issues. You can be short and be sophisticated.

Otherwise, Edward Everett would be a household

name. He gave a two-hour speech on 19 November 1863 in Pennsylvania, USA. The next speaker spoke for barely more than two minutes. Yet chances are you have heard of him and his speech: Abraham Lincoln and the Gettysburg Address.

The power of well-deployed brevity is true outside politics too, which is why Einstein is hailed as a genius for coming up with $E=mc^2$ rather than attacked for dumbing down a core scientific principle to a mere five characters.

And there is the crux of the matter: the art of all effective communication is understanding that your audience sets the terms. Even in the full heat of an election campaign, your audience is only likely to let politics into their lives for a few brief moments. (The same too applies to Einstein, which is why his short formula caught the public's interest in a way that most other Nobel Prize-winning work has never got close to.)

You might think that your original and life-transforming policy ideas deserve more airtime. They cannot be fully appreciated without a lengthy exposition of their merits. By you. From a lectern. Preferably on prime-time TV. But we are talking about effective communication, and communication does not work if your audience is not listening.

Two examples from UK politics illustrate the point well. Margaret Thatcher faced an angry electorate and a restless party when she gave her keynote speech to the Conservative Party conference in 1980. The speech was a long one but it was a single phrase that captured the headlines. 'The lady's not for turning' came to define Margaret Thatcher and her politics in the minds of voters. Another well-chosen phrase defined

New Labour's priorities as they approached their 1997 election victory. In a speech to party members, Tony Blair asked the question: 'What will be our priorities in government?' He answered himself with 'Education, education, education'. The phrase captured both the policy priority and a sense of determination to pursue the agenda.

A sound bite good enough to be remembered does not come easily. What does come easily is always remembering to prioritise. What really is the important message? What would be your first priority if you were (re)elected? Think it, write it and edit it down.

Start by getting your answer to that basic question and go from there. Consider the key issues you will be facing in the campaign and fix on a sound bite that captures what you want to say on each. But of course do not try to use each one every time you speak!

Your sound bites will not only be your message to the public; they will be your reminder to yourself about what you really want to achieve.

CHAPTER 6

STORY TELLING

Facts tell, but stories sell ... If you're not communicating in stories, you're not communicating.
James Carville and Paul Begala

Having persuaded you of the virtues of sound bites in Chapter 5, now we want to persuade you of the virtues of stories.

Story telling makes messages memorable, which means they stick in people's minds. Communications experts Richard Maxwell and Robert Dickman define a story as 'a fact, wrapped in an emotion, that compels us to take an action that transforms our world'.

Not every story quite gets into the world-changing category, but their basic idea is very sound – a story takes a core idea (often thought of as the fable or moral of the story), wraps it in emotion to give it extra impact and then makes it memorable. And stories work better for being short. The Australian Democrats captured the essence with a campaign slogan: 'Keep the bastards honest.' It was a story, a plot and a denouement all in one sentence.

It is not just that the dynamic of a story makes it memorable. Even relatively unexciting stories can work because they also have an internal logic of their own, which means that as you start remembering the first part your brain can work out what the next bit must have been. It is like travelling a route you have taken before – at each step you remember what the next step is. That can turn even a complicated policy or set of arguments into a memorable, moving message.

A great example is the famous 'Daisy Girl' advert run by the Lyndon Johnson US presidential campaign in 1964. It shows a small girl picking the petals off a flower, counting slowly. She stumbles over her counting in a cute way as birds sing in the background. When she gets to nine, an ominous voice takes over, counting down to zero as the camera zooms in on her eye, turning the screen black. As it becomes completely black, it is replaced by images of nuclear Armageddon and a message that the stakes are too high to risk voting for anyone other than Johnson.

Packed into that mini-story is not only a message about foreign policy and nuclear weapons, but also Johnson's experience and judgement compared to that of his opponent, Barry Goldwater, who had made comments about using nuclear weapons in Vietnam.

Like all the best stories it has a beginning (girl picking flowers), a middle (nuclear war) and an end (good news – there is a way to avoid it); you invest emotionally in the central character (the girl); it has a hero (Johnson), a villain (Barry Goldwater) and a happy ending (vote and you save the world). It is like a Spielberg film in miniature, all packed into less than a minute.

The power of the film is even more apparent if you contrast it with what it could have been – a recitation of factual statements and nuclear arsenal statistics. Effective political messages are not made out of bullet points and decimal points, you need stories and emotions.

This film may be the pinnacle of political story making, but the lessons apply even when you are arguing over less weighty issues and on a smaller political stage.

Your stories need to be good and convincing; otherwise, they come across as contrived. Remember what happened in the first televised general election debate in the UK in 2010. All three party leaders had clearly been briefed to wrap their policy points in a human story, 'I was talking to a voter in *X* town last week...' The media and public could not fail to notice, comment and satirise.

But good stories not only help voters to understand how policies might affect them and their lives, they also move the voters to action – to helping and to voting.

CHAPTER 7

BE POPULAR, BUT
BE DISTINCTIVE

What works is being different. Don't try to be liked.
Find out how you're different. Then be that. That's
where the power is. Dave Trott

The idea that the route to electoral success leads candidates to the same middle-of-the-road, identikit spot where everyone looks and sounds much like each other, from the clothes through to the policies, is one of the biggest myths about politics.

It is wrong and it is dangerous. It is dangerous because it breeds a cynicism about politicians ('they're all the same'), and because too many candidates believe that becoming a second-rate clone is what they must do to win.

But it is such a powerful myth because there are a few grains of truth in it. Candidates do need to appeal to a broad range of voters, not just a small group of them. Decades of trial and error and lots of expensive consultancy have taught politicians that there are certain things they can do to broaden their appeal.

However, those grains of truth are not the whole story. Think of the most successful politicians and often you have people who in both their personalities and their policies are very distinctive. Former London mayor Ken Livingstone not only won the 2000 and

2004 contests but also won in 2000 despite being kicked out of his own party. That is an impressive electoral record. Further, not only is he no identikit clone from central candidate casting, in 2000 his headline policy was a radical one that involved making people spend money: introducing congestion charging in London.

In 2008 (and again in 2012), Londoners chose Boris Johnson over Livingstone. Johnson has few discernible features that can be described as 'identikit'. From his unruly hair to his throaty upper-class accent and penchant for making puns in French, he is very much a mould breaker.

Both Ken Livingstone and Boris Johnson made a virtue of being different, not in a contrived way but by playing to the aspects of their personality and politics that made them stand out in a voter-friendly way. Ken wasn't just another politician wanting to be mayor; he was Ken with his congestion charging plan. Boris was a pop star politician who sold his larger-than-life personality as a perfect fit for one of the world's most diverse cities.

The lesson from this for others is not limited to how you look, sound or dress. You can create a powerful and distinctive identity for yourself through the issues you champion, issues on which you clearly differ from an opponent and which are important to the public – so-called 'wedge issues'.

Single-issue campaigning – on issues that resonate with your electorate – is a valuable route to achieving this. Most causes depend on the energetic support of a small number of dedicated people to drive them to success. It can be profitable for the campaigner, too. Look, for example, at Dr Richard Taylor. Taylor, running as an independent, defeated a government minister to win his seat in the UK Parliament in 2001. He then became the first MP in Britain since the Second World War to win as an independent at two general elections, holding his seat in 2005. Taylor was a doctor and campaigned on the issue of protecting local health services, a distinctive cause that he was clearly able to approach with authority. And it was obviously one that struck a chord with voters.

There was also a more subtle cause of Taylor's success – he played up his difference from the political mainstream. He did this in a controlled way that made his message more powerful. Trying too hard to be different in every way can end up blunting your message. Being selective about which differences to stress strengthens it.

'Being different' is sometimes used as an excuse by politicians who do not want to bother with what the public thinks. But for others, being different is a key element of being successful.

CHAPTER 8

YOU ARE HUMAN, NOT A ROBOT

You philosophers are lucky men. You write on paper and paper is patient. I write on the susceptible skins of living beings. Catherine the Great

Although Catherine the Great never had to run for election, she hints at a basic truth that applies to electoral politics. 'Living beings' will not wait for you while you set out, in extensive detail, a comprehensive position paper on your chosen favourite issue.

The default, respectable attitude to have towards politics in public is that it should be about policies not personalities. Personalities seem trivial, demeaning and gossipy while policies are substantive, important and respectable.

It may be a widespread view, but it is wrong. It is wrong for two main reasons, one pragmatic and one principled.

The pragmatic reason is very simple: that is not how voters view politics. Voters do pay attention to personalities and do switch their votes accordingly. In particular voters, consciously or subconsciously, ask themselves this question about candidates, 'Does this person understand and care about people like me?'

That question helps explain why Republican

candidates have often been better at appealing to working-class voters than Democrat candidates in the US, despite their policy platforms being more pro-rich people than those of Democrats. Democrat candidates, like defeated 2004 presidential candidate John Kerry, have come across as not really understanding working-class voters, even if pushing for policies they should like. However unfair the reasons, Kerry was seen as a rather posh snob who understood the lives of rich people and did not understand the lives of ordinary folk.

Conversely, it is why Sarah Palin won such a strong fan base. For many Americans she does come over as understanding them and their lives. (It is a good test of how well someone understands what motivates political support to ask them to explain why Sarah Palin has so many fans. You do not have to like her to be able to answer; but if someone cannot answer other than 'her supporters are bonkers' then you should steer well clear of that person for political advice.)

Indeed, for many voters the details of policies are rather like the MacGuffins in films. This term, popularised by Alfred Hitchcock, can refer to an item around which the plot unfurls. It does not particularly matter what the item is, rather how people react to it. In a spy story quite what the 'big secret' at stake really is does not matter in itself, for the story is about trying to protect or expose a secret. Similarly, it matters for voters how politicians handle an issue rather than the details of the issue itself. Were they decisive? Were they honest?

The principled reason for worrying about personalities in addition to policies is that events frequently justify this. The detailed policies of election manifestos or conference speeches are quickly swept aside by events. Decision making in politics is often messy. Former US Defense Secretary Donald Rumsfeld famously talked about dealing with 'known knowns, known unknowns and unknown unknowns'. Each can blow you off course. Even the local politician has to deal with events, to changes outside of her control that demand judgement and decision making. We may instinctively dislike the notion that politicians are judged by the choices they make in their personal lives but it is understandable that people see it as pretty good shorthand for how sensible they will be in office.

In the UK, former Liberal Democrat leader Charles Kennedy made this point reflecting on Prime Minister Tony Blair's second term in office. The issues on which he, then Conservative leader William Hague and Tony Blair campaigned in 2001 turned out to have very little to do with the major issues that dominated politics in 2001–05. University tuition fees and the war in Iraq were major issues in Parliament but almost completely absent from the 2001 election campaign.

Understanding Tony Blair's personality – and his strong sense of moral duty fuelled by his religious beliefs – would have been a far surer guide to Labour's foreign policy than the details on page 39 of the 2001 Labour manifesto about Labour and the UN. ('We support a more modern and representative Security Council, with more effective peace-keeping', since you ask.)

The most difficult thing about 'selling' your personality is that most people struggle to understand how others perceive their personality. The solution?

Ask people. Ask your friends and colleagues, people you trust to be honest, how they see you, what your strengths and weaknesses are. The best politicians are true to themselves. Work with what you have, rather than trying to fit into an unfamiliar mould.

Remember the wise words of Quintus Cicero to his brother on how to win an election back in ancient Rome: 'Impressing the voters at large ... is done by knowing who people are, being personable and generous, promoting yourself, being available, and never giving up.'

In other words, personalities matter – don't shy away from them and don't act as if they shouldn't.

CHAPTER 9

MAKE PEOPLE BELIEVE
YOU CAN WIN

*If I wanted to persuade people that I could be a good
Member of Parliament, I had better start acting like
one – what I called the 'MP over the water' strategy.*
Paddy Ashdown

Straight after the 1997 general election in the UK,
opinion polls showed that 60 per cent of voters
were Labour supporters. No party has won that many
votes in an election in over a hundred years. Moreover,
the party itself won a bit over two fifths of the votes
cast in the election that had just taken place. Why
did so many people say they backed Tony Blair's party
at that point? There are a number of reasons but a
crucial one you should not under-estimate is that the
new Prime Minister looked like a winner. And looking like a winner can make all the difference to your
prospects in an election contest.

Putting Voters in Their Place, one of our favourite
books, is full of insights into why elections turn out
the way they do. One point authors Ron Johnston and
Charles Pattie make is that people are hugely influenced by their place – that is by what other people
around them (family, neighbours, work colleagues and
so on) are doing. Sometimes it is the herd behaviour
where people copy what others do ('if everyone else is

saying X is great, I don't want to stand out from the crowd'). Sometimes it is based on trust and mental shortcuts ('if my neighbour thinks X is great, I guess they must be'). Sometimes it is the enjoyment of backing the popular or winning choice.

All that goes a long way to explain why getting voters to show they support you is so important.

Voters want to know they are not backing some crazy person whose own mother would not vote for him. More than that, voters love to think they are backing a winner. It is why campaign teams in America invest so heavily in building a sense of momentum behind their candidate. It is why the polls we organised when working for the Liberal Democrats showed party support in marginal contests leaping if people thought the party could win.

So how do you show people that you can win? You need to look popular and look like a winner.

Simple steps like your choice of campaign photos can help. Get photographed with crowds. Be, and appear to be, dynamic. Lonely candidates do not look like winners. Glum candidates do not look like winners.

Build up a store of people who are willing to endorse you. You can use them as 'vox pops' in your campaign literature – real people explaining why you are the best person for the job. If they are 'opinion leaders' with influence over a large network of their own, ask them to be an active advocate.

Look for the places where people are talking about the campaign – online forums for example. Make use of appropriate quotes. Do not be tempted to pretend to be someone else and make up quotes. That is the path to richly deserved disaster.

Looking like a winner is why endorsements and posters should be so important to your campaign plan too (see Chapters 17 and 71).

But looking like a winner is about more than organisational tactics. It is about the language, demeanour and style of being a candidate – confident and leading from the front, both with the public and with your own supporters and helpers. Paddy Ashdown, later to become Liberal Democrat leader, but at the time trying to get into Parliament for a seat where the party was at rock bottom, applied this lesson early on with his 'MP over the water' strategy. He persuaded people he could win by acting as an MP would act – holding advice surgeries around the constituency even though he was but a third-placed candidate, for example. Aside from the direct benefits of helping people, exuding a sense of self-confidence helped persuade people he really could win.

Of course, acting like a winner does not mean taking anything for granted. In many ways the dream election team is a candidate who acts 100 per cent confident of winning and a campaign manager who is 100 per cent paranoid about losing!

CHAPTER 10

UNDERSTAND YOUR OPPONENT

If you know your enemies and know yourself, you can win a hundred battles without a single loss. Sun Tzu

Former US President George W. Bush attracted plenty of ridicule for his mangling of the English language. But when he said that people had 'misunderestimated' him, he had a point.

Listen to many of his political rivals in the run-up to the two presidential elections he fought and they imply they simply could not understand how someone like him could win. He served eight years more as President than any of them managed.

The mistake was that, however much you may passionately believe your opponent is wrong, flawed or a danger, unless you understand them you will not understand their appeal and their campaign.

There are two basic reasons why candidates do this, both perfectly understandable human reactions. First, they are trapped inside politics and second, they are trapped inside themselves.

Normal human beings do not spend every waking hour thinking about politics. We are not the first people to make this point and it will not be the last time we make it in this book. If you analyse your opponent's voter appeal through the prism of full-time politics you will fail to understand them. Just as we have tried to convince you that you need to boil your message down into a digestible chunk that will find a place in voters' crowded lives, so your opponent will do exactly the same.

Voters will not gather information about your opponent in the same obsessive way that you do. If they know anything about the individual at all, it will most likely be what your opponent's campaign has told them (unless your campaign is even pithier, faster and better at describing your opponent to the public).

Voters will not know that your opponent voted the wrong way on the use of natural materials in council properties in the Buildings and Infrastructure sub-committee (and if, by chance, they do, they almost certainly will not care). Do not get trapped inside a political bubble.

When we say candidates get trapped inside themselves we mean that candidates – in fact people in general – tend to take the view that the rest of the world thinks just like them. Of course, they do not.

So what to do?

First, give the job of finding out about your opponent to someone else. Candidates are humans too and hearing how good your opponent is may not be the best way to stay motivated. As long as the person running the campaign understands then that is what is important. Good research will not only help you understand opponents, it will also throw up some gems of facts and quotes that you can use to attack them.

Second, make sure the campaign asks people who are not involved in politics what they think of your opponent. Ideally ask voters in the area you are contesting and ask them in a structured way (through polling or surveying).

Third, act on it.

One of the most common mistakes made by politicians who have been defeated by Liberal Democrat challengers is to decry their opponents' concentration on street-level politics such as getting potholes fixed or bus routes improved. Describing these issues, in mocking tones, as not being proper politics worthy of parliamentarians, they failed to understand the appeal of the campaign they were up against. Whether or not you agree with it, you need to understand it to know how you should handle it.

Do not become obsessed with your opponent's every move but do not 'misunderestimate' them either. After all, is your election-winning record better than that of former governor and two-term President George W. Bush?

CHAPTER 11

TEST, TEST, TEST

Insanity: doing the same things over and over and expecting different results. Albert Einstein

Remember New Coke? If you were a fizzy drink consumer in the late 1980s, you will. The global mega brand launched a new version of Coca-Cola to much fanfare but it turned into a marketing disaster and, in the end, the original recipe Coke was restored to the shelves. A costly mistake that boiled down to a failure in market testing: the researchers had tested what people thought of the new taste after a few sips, without understanding how the negative views of others could change that initial response.

Idealistic political activists are often weary and wary of comparisons between politics and product sales but we are here to tell you, loud and proud, that there is much for successful campaigners to learn from the world of business. Testing your product, checking the results and re-testing it are vital components in a successful campaign. If you do not believe us, think about the alternative – not testing, not analysing, not adapting – and ponder the words of Albert Einstein at the top of this page.

Mark runs an email newsletter. An edition sent out at the worst time of day and day of week gets only half the readership of one sent out at the best time and on the best day. That is a massive difference – learning when is a good time and when is a bad time does the equivalent of doubling (or halving) the size of the email list.

However, the best and worst times are not the same on this newsletter list as on others. The only way to learn this is to test, measure and test again. Experience may give you a shrewd idea of what the most likely options are to test first, but even experience is not infallible. As Mark Twain put it, 'The trouble with the world is not that people know too little, but that they know so many things that ain't so.'

By no means all aspects of political campaigning are as easy to test as changing the email send time and checking the open rate. Sometimes the testing may be a little rough round the edges and involve rather more in the way of instinctive judgements. That is not just a problem for political campaigners: look at the example of New Coke again. The Coca-Cola Company has been around for 120 years and has an annual turnover similar to the country of Luxembourg. It did not get that way by failing to test its products with consumers. It seems that the fatal mistake made with New Coke was a failure to understand what the tests were saying. Straightforward taste tests said consumers liked it. A small number of people reacted negatively when told it was Coke but in a focus group environment those people had a major impact on other people. Their vocal opposition to the new brand put others off the product and that is exactly what happened when the product launched.

So the lesson is not to solely look at one set of results but to try to understand what the results are telling you and the best way to do that is to test what you are doing in a variety of ways.

The benefits are great when you introduce a culture of test, test and test all the way through the campaign organisation. If you are running a street stall to collect petition signatures, for example, you might have figured out that you collect more on a particular day of the week. But have you trialled the success of wearing badges and stickers that illustrate who you are campaigning for? Does this help or hinder in getting more petition signatures? Does it result in a better response from the public?

Testing what works best can save you valuable time and money. Few campaigners have enough of either and cannot afford to waste what they have. You do not have to be Einstein but your campaign will benefit if you allow a little bit of his thinking into it.

CHAPTER 12

SET THE AGENDA

Make others dance to your tune.

The UK's voting reform referendum in May 2011 deserves close examination by anyone interested in how to win (or lose) elections. The 'no' campaign achieved a spectacular victory despite early polls showing support for the two sides to be evenly balanced.

The 'no' campaign was incredibly successful in defining the territory on which the campaign was fought. As a result, the unfortunate 'yes' campaign devoted far too much time and resources to rebutting claims about the fairness, efficacy and cost of the proposed new system of electing Members of Parliament. Moreover, the 'no' campaign made the contest about the pros and cons of the proposed new system rather than about the pros and cons of the system it would replace – a classic case of setting the agenda.

The 'no' campaign achieved this by doing two things. First, it found out which of its campaign messages worked best with voters (by asking them). Then it ruthlessly pushed those messages out using the means it had available. The opposing 'yes' campaign fell into the trap and took on the spadework for their opponents by repeating the 'no' attacks in order to rebut them. It was a textbook example of a campaign being blown off its agenda and dancing to someone else's tune.

We look at how to deal with negative campaigning in Chapter 15 but, whether your opponents' messages are positive or negative, your first objective should be to make them talk about your agenda not the other way round.

Election contests mix two types of struggles: which issues are important (does the environment matter?); who can best handle universally agreed important issues (who will deliver the best health services?).

In most elections you, and your opponent, will have different strengths and weaknesses. You will each want to emphasise different issues to highlight your positives and your opponent's negatives. So setting the election agenda, setting the terms of the debate, can play a critical part in deciding the outcome.

It is not easy to achieve but there are three things you should do to make sure the debate is on your territory:

- Make sure you know what you want the issues to be.
- Get in early and often with your arguments. Tell the people who will be talking about the election what the election is about (your preferred issues of course).
- Avoid dancing to other people's tunes by always responding to what your opponent does or says.

It also means following the advice of Norwegian Erik Solheim: 'The only way to control your content is to be the best provider of it.' In other words, you cannot stop other people talking about you, your policies or the issues. The better you are at providing information – the clearer, the more plausible, the more timely it is – the more people will look to your information and your version of events. That way your opponents end up talking about the election on your terms.

We worked on a winning campaign where part of our candidate's message was to attack the incumbent's work rate. It was mediocre and deserved criticism, and the incumbent failed to find an effective line of defence. Instead of talking positively about what they were doing in Parliament the campaign descended into an 'oh yes I am, oh no you're not' debate about whether the incumbent was working hard enough. Our opponent had lost the agenda, and that helped them to lose the election.

If you do not set the agenda, your opponent will – and they will not pick the agenda you want.

CHAPTER 13

PRIORITISE YOUR ISSUES

If everything is important, nothing is important.

Polls commissioned by Conservative peer Michael Ashcroft in the run-up to the 2005 general election, showed that, each day, between 73 per cent and 83 per cent of the public could not remember having heard anything about the Conservative Party recently. On only four occasions was any one activity or message noticed by more than one in twenty (5 per cent) of people – and that was for a national political party, running a national campaign. Even in times of intense political news coverage, much of it passes by most people. For individual candidates it is so much tougher.

With so little attention, every little bit really has to count. A campaigner cannot communicate every possible issue at once. You need to pick and prioritise.

There can be a tension between which issues you think matter most and which issues matter most to voters. It is important for you to make the space for the issues you care about most. Candidates are often at their most convincing when they are talking about an issue they know and about which they are truly passionate. But it is also important to grasp where that issue fits in the list of campaign priorities and how best to highlight it.

Real problems can arise if a campaign fails to prioritise at all. Trying to say too many different things will result in people having no clear idea what you are saying about anything.

The best way to make it count is to focus on a small number of issues rather than saying something different each time you get the public's attention.

This was the strategy adopted successfully in 2007 by Australian Labor Party leader Kevin Rudd. Although he deeply disliked the incumbent government, he chose to disagree publicly with them on only a small number of issues. As a result, the media attention in the campaign focused on those areas of difference, areas deliberately chosen by the Rudd campaign to play to its strengths.

When choosing your priorities, remember to ask what your choice of issues says about you. British politician Lembit Öpik is well known for his colourful lifestyle and appearances on celebrity television. He was also an effective advocate and single-issue campaigner. However, we cannot help feeling that his choice of issues would have created a poor impression among his electorate. The threat of asteroid strikes, the use of electric bicycles and the disappearance of spaghetti pesto from Parliament's restaurant menus all have their merits as causes. Voters, however, prefer their representative to focus on issues such as health care, taxes, education and the state of the economy.

Liberal Democrat campaign guru and peer Chris Rennard developed the 'three Es' for one election (education, environment and electoral reform). Similarly, Australian spin-doctor Lynton Crosby encouraged the Conservatives to adopt a 'ten-word campaign' in 2005.

How you identify the priority issues is important, too. First and foremost is the ability to listen to your electorate. We talk elsewhere about the mechanics of gathering the views of voters (see Chapter 80, for example). But the fundamental point needs little science: if you want to be listened to, you need to talk about things voters are interested to hear.

All of that is not to say you should only talk about the same narrow set of issues in the same way all of the time. It means you should identify the issues that are most important to your campaign and give repeated prominence to them. If you can capture them in a simple theme that defines the purpose of your campaign, so much the better ('it's the economy, stupid!'). Choose the right issues for the right audiences (this is most certainly not the same as saying conflicting things to different people).

Always remember how crowded the lives of your voters are and how little space they can allow for politics. Within that space, they want to hear your views on the issues that matter most to them.

CHAPTER 14

STAYING ON MESSAGE IS NOT
THE SAME AS REPETITION

The absolute rule of message dissemination and message penetration is consistency and repetition. Mary Matalin

We like repetition. Repetition is good. Repetition reinforces your key message in an age where you are competing for voters' attention in an information-saturated world, especially when you are dealing with politics – a topic most people pay little attention to most of the time (did we mention that already?). American Democrat political consultant Al From coined the phrase 'low information rationality' to describe this: people are not dumb, but they do make political decisions based on not very much information.

You need to love repetition to get a message across.

But underneath the repetition of a few key messages there needs to be some substance. Otherwise a candidate can be left looking insubstantial, even less than honest.

Look at what happened to Labour Party leader Ed Miliband when one of his interviews 'went viral' on the internet. 'Going viral' on YouTube can be an ad man's dream but it can also be the stuff of nightmares.

In the summer of 2011, Ed Miliband gave a TV interview that did nothing to enhance his reputation. Asked about his view on public sector strikes, he gave a decent first answer. So far, so good. What went wrong was the second, third, fourth and further answers – which were all almost exactly the same. It left Ed Miliband looking like a robot.

Of course, most candidates will not enjoy the same media exposure as the leader of a national political party but most successful campaigns will attract scrutiny. Whether it is through media interviews, public debates or even just meeting voters on the doorstep, appearing to have only one thing to say will damage your credibility. Moreover, the internet increases scrutiny at all levels.

The best campaigns are dynamic – re-playing a core message in numerous different forms over time. Engaging voters rather than boring them to death.

Whether it is for home broadband or instant coffee, commercial advertisers have known for years the power of developing a story to reinforce a single basic message. And developing the story works best when you build it around characters that people can relate to. (The makers of a particularly successful brand of instant mashed potato in the 1970s will tell you that the characters do not even have to be human but we struggled to find the campaigning message in that!)

A good example is UK politician Lynne Featherstone, who won election to Parliament in 2005 in part thanks to presenting herself successfully as an expert on crime. This let her showcase her own expertise (she had served on London's top policing body for several years) and appeal to voters on an issue near the top of their list of concerns. She did this by having one well-tuned core phrase – 'Lynne has served on London's top policing body' – which was repeated heavily, and by talking about numerous local crime issues of concern to people: encouraging Neighbourhood Watches, campaigning for a local police station to get its front counter back, lobbying for more police patrols and so on.

The message was the same but the demonstration of the message varied. Voters were not bored by mindless repetition but they were persuaded by a strong and consistent message, illustrated in a range of ways. This approach not only keeps the message fresh, it also increases the chances for each voter that at least one of the illustrations really chimes with their personal experiences. Vary the demonstration but stick to the message.

CHAPTER 15

DEALING WITH
NEGATIVE CAMPAIGNING

You shouldn't judge a nation by their politicians. After all, the English, on the whole, are an honest people.
Miss Froy, *The Lady Vanishes* (1938)

There are two great 'bar room truths' in political campaigning. One, that politics should be about policies not personalities, we dismissed in Chapter 8. The other is that before politics was ruined by negative campaigning there was a long-lost golden age.

In fact as any student of nineteenth-century electioneering will tell you, negative campaigning has a long, long history. The sort of religious hatred that passed for the norm in election literature then makes comments on many political blogs now seem quite tame by comparison. And as the quote above shows, the public has long been sceptical of politicians' positive self-image!

Campaigners are drawn to negative messages because they are effective (just ask a string of defeated Democrat presidential candidates in the United States how effective they are). They can switch voters away from a candidate and they can demotivate a candidate's supporters. But they are also an established part of elections for another reason.

The important point is that politicians should be held to account for their errors and misjudgements. They should not get away with presenting a glossed-over image of their own achievements if the reality is somewhat different. That means you have to understand the power of negative campaigning and be prepared for it to make an appearance in any election contest.

Let us illustrate.

Mark once produced leaflets for a council election highlighting the council's failure to check properly the background of its staff who came into close and regular contact with children. As a result of this failure a convicted sex offender was employed in a job that he should not have been.

There were complaints about negative campaigning. But what was worse? Pointing out to the public the mistakes the council was making so people could judge their importance or drawing a public veil of silence over the failures?

Simply put, the public has a right to know the full story – and the public is quite capable of judging how relevant an issue is to their choice of vote.

When you are on the receiving end of negative campaigning, you need to decide whether to respond.

The effectiveness of any message is a function of its reach (how many people absorb it) and its impact (how important it is to them in deciding who to vote for.) You need to remember this when you decide whether to respond to an attack. Assess four things:

How many voters saw the attack (remember, not everyone reads every leaflet or sees every ad)?

How many times will your opponents be able to repeat it?

Is it an issue that people care about?

Does it 'go with the grain', i.e. does it reinforce existing pre-conceptions?

A good example of this is the reaction to the UK coalition government's attempts to reform the National Health Service following the 2010 general election. Health care is a hugely important issue to most people. The reform process took months as the legislation went through Parliament, giving opponents ample opportunity to repeat attacks through the media. And the attack chimed with an existing weakness for the Conservative Party – that they could not be trusted to protect the NHS.

There is a real skill in rebutting claims without simply repeating them, because if you repeat them you give them more coverage and risk people thinking 'there's no smoke without fire'.

In one council by-election campaign, Mark faced just this problem after a sitting councillor resigned. The other parties claimed the councillor was not fully committed to the area, not working hard enough and so on. The response was a personal letter from the retiring councillor thanking residents for their many good wishes after her two recent hospital operations. True – and a very effective way of making attacks look very churlish and mean without repeating them.

The response may have been indirect but it tackled the central accusation head on, on the candidate's terms rather than on the terms of the attackers.

The best way to prepare for negative campaigning is to assess your own weaknesses before the campaign begins. Do not shy away from them. Work out what they are and how you are going to address them – where possible get your rebuttal in first (so that you can do it on your own terms). Do not go over the top – do not make your weaknesses the centrepiece of your campaign – but do deal with weaknesses rapidly, rationally and clearly.

The worst way to react to negative campaigning (or any sort of unfortunate event that is beyond your immediate control) is to do nothing and then to moan about it. Decide whether to respond or ignore and then act firmly on that decision.

As one of our friends, another seasoned professional campaigner, puts it: victims do not win.

CHAPTER 16

DEFINE THE ELECTION AS BEING FOR A JOB YOUR CANDIDATE AND ONLY YOUR CANDIDATE CAN DO

If the job definition has your name in it, you win.

John Major's victory in the 1992 general election was one of the biggest surprises in post-war UK electoral history. He had come to power two years earlier following a 'palace coup' against Margaret Thatcher, with the government facing huge public opposition to its local government finance reforms. Even on the eve of polling day, the Labour opposition was confident of victory. One factor that explains Major's success was the ability of his campaign to define the 'job description' for the role for which he and Labour leader Neil Kinnock were competing. At a time of considerable economic difficulties, Major convinced the electorate that he had the skills to manage the economy effectively and that Kinnock did not.

Five years later, John Major failed to repeat the trick because what people expected of their Prime Minister had shifted towards management of effective public services in a more positive economic climate (it did not help either that Major had struggled to look like an effective manager of either the economy or his party after his earlier election victory). In 2010, Gordon Brown attempted to convince voters that it would be dangerous to switch to an inexperienced alternative. In that election the Conservative opposition had no difficulty in convincing voters it was time for a change though they failed to convince enough of them that their man was the only one equipped to deliver that change.

A winning campaign needs to convince voters that the post you are competing for is one that you, and only you, can do. When it comes to casting its vote, the public not only needs to decide it wants to vote for you, it needs to decide it wants to vote for you ahead of the other options available. Liking you is not enough; you must be preferable to the other candidates on the ballot paper.

It is not only about the abstract merits of each candidate, it is also about framing the choice as being one where your strengths and advantages are just what is needed.

If those lie in foreign policy knowledge, then it is in getting the public to agree that foreign policy expertise is crucial. But if they lie in health service expertise, then you need to persuade the public that the contest is about choosing who can make the better decisions over health policy.

Candidates and their campaigns often forget this key point: that however experienced you may be you need to be seen as the best in the area. Take the example of Jimmy Carter's changing fortunes in the 1976 and 1980 American presidential elections. In 1976, amid the back-wash of the Watergate scandal, Carter's outsider image and home-spun solutions appeared perfect for dealing with home-grown problems. In

1980, after an oil price shock, the Soviet invasion of Afghanistan and the Iranian revolution, Carter was judged ill fit to deal with an agenda dominated by external threats. In 1976, the idea of a President carrying his own suitcase on to Air Force One suited the needs of the time for a humble outsider; by 1980 it was a damaging image of someone not up to serious action on the world stage.

So look carefully through the possible strengths of the different candidates or likely candidates and make sure you present the contest as being one that needs the strengths you – and only you – can bring to the job.

CHAPTER 17

THIRD-PARTY ENDORSEMENTS

*Of course a politician says they're amazing, but if
someone you know says so...*

Imagine you read in a newspaper or hear on the
radio a candidate saying how good they are. Do
they convince you? Even if they have the oratorical
skills of a Winston Churchill, no, because of course
someone is going to say they think well of themselves.

What carries real weight is when it is other people
awarding the praise – which is why third-party
endorsements are so often highly prized by candidates.

A good place to start is with your own party, if you
have one. Party members praising each other can be
nearly as weak as someone praising themselves. But
if they are people with a particularly high profile
and popularity, even if in just one community, then
their backing can carry a great deal of weight with
those within that community, whether the link be
geographic, religious, ethnic or something else.

Recognisable non-party public figures add two
advantages as endorsers – they are known to a wider
group of people and their independence makes their
endorsements more powerful. They can be hard to
secure, which is why good campaigners identify
possible backers well in advance of an election and
make sure they all get personally contacted to try to

persuade them to back the candidate and make an endorsement. That can take some time – and more than one round of personal contact – so starting early is necessary.

Endorsements from firefighters and military figures were especially powerful in the US after 9/11, for example – the individuals may not have been well known but their uniforms identified them and gave them great credibility. Celebrities from the entertainment world can be more problematic (perhaps because they often lack the credibility factor) but used in the right way they can have a positive effect. Barack Obama's email invitation to buy a chance of dinner with himself and George Clooney, for example, was a big hit at encouraging people to give money to his campaign.

The most powerful endorsers are those who are also the hardest to use: friends and neighbours of your voters. These people can have a powerful effect but the number they can influence is usually far smaller than public figures. It is difficult to work out exactly who knows who and therefore who should receive which particular personally endorsed leaflet or letter.

As a result campaigns often take a simple geographic approach – get at least one endorser for each recognisable community or clutch of streets and use their name on the leaflets or letters that go out in that area. The smaller the geographic areas, the greater the impact – but the more organisation required. Once again, starting early is important. Remember, however, that geography is not the only way to reach voters and for many people an endorser who lives far away but who shares some attribute or interest with them will carry more weight than a resident from a neighbouring road.

It is important that an endorsement comes with credibility. If you decide to publicise that someone is supporting you it is important to check that person is someone whose endorsement helps your campaign. Do they have credibility? Do they share your values?

The rise of social media has made identifying such grassroots supporters easier as fans on a Facebook page, followers on Twitter and so on make for good lists of people to ask. Of course, not everyone on such a list will actually be a supporter, and not everyone who is will be happy to have their name used, but they are a good place to start the hunt.

By whatever route you find the names, make sure that names are found and then used. Nothing beats the personal endorsement.

CHAPTER 18

ONE CAMPAIGN, ONE MESSAGE

Be consistent across different communication channels.

The audience is the most important part of communication. A successful campaign will recognise that different audiences consume information in different ways. It is why there are newspapers as different as *The Times* and *The Sun*. It is why social networking sites do not read like sales letters from the *Reader's Digest*.

Different communication channels require different skills. Someone who excels at writing direct mail messages may not be any good at sorting out the data for direct mail let alone at filming YouTube clips or advising people what approaches work best when talking to voters on the doorstep.

As a result, campaigns often – and rightly – end up with different people specialising in different media. That works well if you are making use of different specialist skills to make for a more effective campaign. It does not work well if you end up with different people saying different things in different places.

Not surprisingly, good communication is the key to an effective communications strategy. Simple methods can be used to set up the framework for people to work in. Real examples will be a useful guide.

Careful checking, regular discussion and constructive feedback will help ensure everyone understands the key messages, their role and the objectives of the campaign.

Produce one 'message sheet' that summarises the main messages to use, the key slogans and pieces of evidence to cite and so on. Work with the people who best understand their media to decide how to get those messages across most effectively. Then everyone involved in producing communications that may be read, seen or heard by the public should be given the sheet, have its logic explained to them and be kept updated with any changes. It is particularly important to explain any subtlety of language that must be correct in order to ensure statements are factually accurate.

The output needs checking – as indeed it often needs to be for legal and other reasons. Consistency should occur if you combine the initial advice with the checking afterwards.

If the key messages are short and clear (as they should be!) then they can work across different media, as the 'Kevin '07' slogan and messages showed very successfully for then Australian Labor Party leader Kevin Rudd. From speeches to printed literature, T-shirts, interviews and the online world, there was a consistent and very disciplined image and presentation of Kevin Rudd. In his case this was all the more important because his campaign deliberately wanted to stress only a few differences from the government – keeping the differences to a small number forced the media to talk about them as they were the only major talking points. The reality did not always quite meet the theory but it worked well, producing a message that was both consistent and tailored to the different channels.

It can sound hard work to ensure such specialism and consistency – and it is. Some of Ed's best experiences involve working with a couple of gnarled old newspaper hacks who volunteered to help on the production of campaign material. One, a former reporter, refused to write headlines and the other, a former sub-editor, refused to write copy but together they produced material with real impact.

Nevertheless, the benefit of a consistent message applied successfully to suit the quirks of each communication channel is that the overall campaign is more than the sum of its parts, rather than one that collapses under contradictory messages.

CHAPTER 19

BE FLEXIBLE

No battle plan survives contact with the enemy.
Helmuth von Moltke

An old saying claims you learn more from your defeats than your victories. But a winning campaign we were both involved in educated us more than a university library.

The Dunfermline by-election victory for the Liberal Democrats in February 2006 was an extraordinary affair. The campaign began with the party engaged in a leadership contest following Charles Kennedy's admission of problems with alcohol. It descended into farce as two leadership contenders encountered difficulties with their personal lives. With the Scottish National Party chomping at the bit to take on Labour in its stronghold and Lib Dem poll ratings diving, our candidate, Willie Rennie, seemed more likely to finish fourth than first.

There are a number of reasons why Willie snatched a dramatic victory, not least his strong roots in the area, but his flexibility was vital.

In the first instance, it was the flexibility to recognise that an off-the-shelf campaign would not strike a chord with the electorate. Instead, the candidate and the campaign team identified their own set of campaign priorities after listening to voters.

Secondly, the campaign staff were smart enough to recognise the importance of local knowledge. One large village on the edge of the constituency in particular was marked out early on as a weak spot that would not warrant much attention. Local members thought otherwise and pressed for the campaign to take the area seriously. Sure enough, the early canvass data that came back was strong and voters there responded positively to the full-scale campaign that then followed.

Thirdly, of course, the campaign had to learn how to deal with the news that kept coming out of London. It was so awful that, in the HQ at least, the response was a lot of gallows humour. On the street, though, the team learned quickly that voters were much less concerned with the 'Westminster bubble' than they were with getting a decent deal on local public services.

Most candidates will not have to campaign in such a crazy atmosphere but there are still important lessons for all campaigns.

Some occasions where you have to be flexible are obvious, such as an outside event intruding on the campaign, shooting an issue up the political agenda. Judging how to respond is more difficult but the best answer is (as always) to talk to some voters to find out their views on the issue.

Harder to judge, normally, are the occasions when it is a question of how well your opponent is doing. Do you need to change your plans to respond to the success of their campaign?

Spotting that your opponent is having an impact and working out how to respond is difficult – it does not have a one-size-fits-all answer. Calm, rational thought and the avoidance of panic are at a premium at such times. There is no substitute for real data too.

You will not always be as lucky as Mark on one occasion during a by-election. He was out delivering leaflets when he spotted the opposition candidate having their photo taken. Keeping his ears open as he went passed, he realised they were taking photos about a local traffic speeding issue – one on which the opponent's party had previously promised action but not taken any. Expecting that a new set of promises would soon be made, Mark rushed back to the campaign HQ and put together a leaflet on the issue, reminding residents about the past broken promises and warning people to therefore watch out for any new election time pledges. The leaflet was then delivered in the area before the opposition leaflet appeared! However the information gets to you, always be prepared to learn from what you are being told – and remember the bigger picture. Switching tactics and details in changed circumstances is sensible flexibility; changing strategy and direction in response to every passing event is not.

As the entrepreneur Seth Godin puts it, 'Plans are great. But missions are better. Missions survive when plans fail, and plans almost always fail.'

At such times everyone needs to be very clear who is making the final decision and, when it is made, what it is and the importance of sticking to it. Protracted agonising and inconsistency comes at a big price, even if the right decision is reached in the end.

Your opponents are unlikely to lie down and let you win. So no matter how well planned your campaign is, with carefully organised logistics and well-formed messages, some things will need to change during the campaign. When they do, remember Germaine Greer's wise words – 'act quickly, think slowly'. Make decisions calmly and carry out any necessary changes swiftly.

CHAPTER 20

THE POWER OF IMAGES

A picture is not worth a thousand words.

The old cliché – that a picture is worth a thousand words – is rather misleading. The most powerful and memorable words trump pictures repeatedly. That is why the vast majority of the most memorable events in politics are words, not pictures: Winston Churchill's speeches during the Second World War, for example, or JFK's inaugural address.

Move down into the more humdrum world of an election campaign, however, and photographs *can* trump words. The very best words trump a photo, but even a mediocre photo can trump all but the very best words.

Even a quick glance at a mediocre photograph can convey so much information and emotion. In a world where the public often does not spend much time thinking about politics, cherish and exploit this speed of transmission.

To do this well, precede the use of photographs – and other visual images – with these questions: 'what information do I want to convey?' and 'what emotions do I want to invoke?'

Getting the answers to these questions right determines the political impact of the eventual image far more than the technical skill of the photographer or the quality of the equipment used. Both of those certainly help, and avoid unfocused or badly framed photos, but take the right sort of image in the first place.

For example, the Labour Party used photographs after the Second World War to remind people powerfully of the horrors of mass unemployment in Britain before 1939. As one Conservative agent complained at the time, Labour made 'very effective use of photographs showing unemployment between the wars. We relied solely on figures and graphs.'

It does not always work. In 2008, one US Democrat congressman, Tim Mahoney, applied this thinking to a campaign mailing using photos of soldiers and a veteran proudly displaying his medals next to the headline 'Honoring those who defend our freedom'. The idea was a good one – save that the veteran was not an American but a Russian. As a Republican spokesman put it, 'Is Tim Mahoney's commitment to our veterans so shallow and superficial that he can't even tell the difference between an American veteran and one who fought for Communism in Joseph Stalin's Red Army?'

Of course, most likely, a junior staff member made a mistake with a photo library, but the buck rightly stops with the candidate, especially if they are in the photograph. Then Liberal Party leader Jo Grimond discovered this the hard way when the photograph for one of his campaign stops went horribly wrong – he was snapped not with the Liberal candidate but with the incumbent Labour MP!

Think carefully about the message the photo *really* sends. It is common to see in local-level political leaflets photographs showing a candidate standing on their own (often pointing at something in the distance). Yet we have never come across a campaign where the right message is presenting the candidate as a lonely soul. A solo photo can work – but only rarely and only if you have the right appearance and pose. A favourite of ours is of Ronald Reagan sitting, relaxed, on a stage at a campaign meeting. Reagan has his legs crossed, exposing the sole of his shoe. The sole is worn through, sending powerful messages about Reagan's work ethic and his common touch.

For far more than the quality of the image, what matters is the choice, with the emotional message that it sends. Strong, popular, dynamic, successful – those are the messages you want to convey.

PART 2

THE TEAM

Once you have a message, you need to be able to communicate it and this requires a team and resources. In this section, we explain how to build up a large, skilled and effective team before turning to the question of other resources in Part 3.

Successful campaigns are never a solo effort: even the least sophisticated campaigns draw on a range of different abilities. But creating, motivating and growing a team demands a special skill. The best candidates understand the importance of building a big team and know how to make it happen.

CHAPTER 21

WHY YOU NEED A TEAM

Many hands make light work.

There is a simple reason why making a success of teams is so important: teams do not magically materialise overnight even in a work environment where people can be given instructions. In a political campaign, with its heavy reliance on volunteers, building successful teams requires all the more work.

As we take you through the necessary roles for leadership, different types of teams, how to motivate people, how to make teams work well and so on, it is worth remembering the four key reasons for bothering with teams at all.

However efficient you are and however hardworking you are, you still only have twenty-four hours in a day and seven days in a week. Teams mean more people getting more work done.

It is not just about the work that more people can do; more people bring more knowledge, more experience and more perspectives. With good management you can avoid falling into indecisive discursiveness and make more well-informed decisions – and therefore better ones.

Moreover, good teams provide resilience. Not only will things go wrong, so too will people. Whether it is someone not up to the job or an event such as a family bereavement quite rightly taking someone away from the campaign, there will be circumstances where another person needs to fill the gap. Changing circumstances will also put extra demands on parts of the team as events, the campaign and politics more generally play out. Bigger and better teams are more resilient in such circumstances.

Finally, and perhaps most importantly, teams make for a better politics. The more people actively involved in a democracy, the healthier it is. Building teams is one of those thankful occasions when self-interest in winning and wider interest in the public good both point you in exactly the same direction.

Successful teams have good leadership; leadership that helps, supports and guides people but which also lets them get on with their jobs. As once said in the magazine *Campaigns & Elections*, you should never put a steering committee behind the steering wheel. Nor should you leave the steering wheel unattended. One leads to paralysis, the other to crashes. We are not fans of either.

What we are fans of is having a team – and one big enough to win. Follow this rule of thumb: there should be one helper for every 200 electors.

That 1:200 ratio (call it the Maxfield–Pack Ratio, or MPR, if you like) comes from experience in many elections at many different levels and includes everyone from leaflet deliverer through to office workers. In practice, a large number of the team are likely to be your leaflet deliverers, but one reason we like the ratio is that it is a healthy reminder that leaflet deliverers (who can on average cover far more than 200 electors each) are not the be-all and end-all of a team. You need plenty more people to cover plenty of other tasks.

So work out your optimum team size by using the MPR and keep it constantly in mind. If the team is too small, then increasing its size should always be a priority. Otherwise you end up trying to run a campaign on a scale that cannot cope with what you should be doing.

CHAPTER 22

GRASSROOTS TEAMS

They're good for you, they're good for politics.

Building a central team with volunteers regularly coming into the campaign HQ to help is good. Grassroots teams are, however, even better, with people carrying out campaigning in their own communities and their own streets. Even the best of central teams cannot match the combination of local knowledge and direct local contact that grassroots teams provide. You need people on the ground noticing information and you need people on the ground persuading their neighbours, colleagues and families to support your message.

Having volunteers on the ground risks the old problem of 'out of sight, out of mind', particularly when it comes to remembering to look after them, thank them and keep them supplied with useful and interesting tasks at times that suit when they want to help. This means you need volunteer team managers whose role is to maintain the volunteer network.

Building genuine grassroots teams is one of the toughest organising jobs there is. Thankfully, the benefits are immense in terms of getting more done and getting better feedback about what is happening – not to mention the advantage of the more people working on the campaign, the more voters may know one of them, contributing to that crucially influential indirect personal endorsement.

It is also important to build diverse teams. One of the most common problems that growing organisations face is breaking the habit of recruiting people who remind them of themselves. It is often a subconscious move – your own habits will lead you to look in particular places for people to recruit to the team. We have worked with candidates who are middle-aged men whose core team consisted of other middle-aged men. We have worked with young women who had a fantastic ability to recruit other young women to the campaign.

However, truly successful campaigns will aim to recruit from a whole range of backgrounds. Often the key to achieving that will be to involve a wide range of people in recruiting to the team. Identify the people you already have in the team who have the skills or background that you are looking for more of. Find out what motivates them to be involved and use that to recruit others. Ask them if they would be willing to do the recruiting for you, among their friends, colleagues or among specially targeted groups of voters.

When building grassroots teams, expect that there will be quite a high dropout rate between people first expressing a possible interest in helping and becoming regular, reliable helpers. You can minimise the dropouts by asking for help in a skilled way (Chapter 26) and remembering to say thank you (Chapter 29). Another good tip is to ask for feedback (perhaps via an anonymous survey) from people who drop out, such as leaflet deliverers who stop. That may identify problems you were not aware of – perhaps an organiser was too abrupt with people.

When people start helping ensure you provide them with plenty of training and motivation. Offer training diplomatically: there are useful tips for even the apparently simplest of tasks – the difference between putting a piece of paper through a letterbox with a draught excluder well and doing it badly is immense! Explain not just the technical skills but also provide motivation. Let the team know how what they do forms part of a desirable bigger vision (see Chapter 24).

Make sure someone is always keeping an eye out for those keen team members, those who do less or those who want to do something different. Reducing the amount that people are asked to do, when appropriate, helps keep someone from dropping out. Watching out for when they might want to do more or do something different also helps turn the grassroots helpers into a 'talent system' for people who might end up taking on more senior and more responsible roles in the campaign.

Above all be clear, be consistent and – politely – set deadlines.

CHAPTER 23

LEADING THE TEAM

There may be no I in team but there is ME.

You know the old saying, there is no 'I' in team. However, you do not have to be much of a linguistic detective to spot the flaw in this appeal against egotism, for the letters 'm' and 'e' are there. That should not just please contrarians, it should also please those who want successful teams, for successful teams not only involve everyone making their own contribution, they also involve successful leadership.

Search for leadership on Google and you get nearly 500 million results. There are enough practical insights and cod theories out there to keep you going through to your next election and beyond. Look for guidance on leading teams of volunteers, though, and the virtual bookshelves are almost bare (three, to be precise, when we tried it). So, in best 'airport book' style, here are our top ten tips for leading a volunteer team:

1. Lead by example. Work hard and 'get dirt under your nails' helping with the tasks that you expect others to do for the campaign.
2. Remember they are volunteers. They got involved because they shared your vision, so make the campaign about them as much as it is about you.

3. Communicate your vision clearly. Do not keep the plans to a tiny cabal. Consult regularly and explain often the direction you want the team to go and how you want them to get there.

4. Good leadership is not the same as hubris or arrogance. Good leaders know that they learn from experience and from others in the team. Make sure there is a way that people can express their views and make it clear that those views are being listened to (the core leadership team needs to be lean and efficient but, for example, have one regular stream of meetings that are big and inclusive so that a wider group can have their say).

5. Encourage learning, communication and sharing throughout the organisation. The team should reflect the leadership culture throughout. If it is to be effective, it will have a number of people in leadership positions. It is your job to make sure they understand how to lead in the right way.

6. Have patience. People are busy, they get distracted, they do not always agree with you. You will have to explain things more than once.

7. Have a strategy for effective decision making. Meetings are sure to play an important part. As author and management expert Roy Lilley puts it, 'Meetings are management.' Have an agenda, turn up and start on time, keep to time during the meeting (do not let huge amounts of time be spent on item one and then rush items two to seven) and send round clear action points promptly after the end of the meeting.

8. Be consistent. This is not the same as being inflexible but be true to your values. Do not be

tempted to evade confrontation by saying one thing to one person and another to another. Have tactical flexibility but once you have set out the big vision make sure you live by it. You may not convince everyone but you will win their respect and your supporters will stay motivated.

9. Treat volunteers like humans. It is often a telling sign to watch a candidate pass through a group of helpers in a campaign HQ on their way to a meeting room or their office. Do they smile, briefly chat and say thanks or do they dash through, head down off to their terribly important meeting? Charismatic candidates have a 'look at me' quality but the best candidates are able to convey the message, 'look at me, but I am more interested in you'.

10. Understand that good teams embrace a wide range of skills and personalities. Do not expect everyone to follow you like sheep. Encourage challenges (in the right setting – those naturally inclined to challenge need to understand that challenge done inappropriately can demotivate and will not help them get their way).

Get these ten steps right and you will find your team growing in size and dedication.

CHAPTER 24

SMALL STEPS, BIG VISION

A political party is about more than plans and priorities and policies in a chromium-plated organisation. It also has a heart and a history and a soul. Paddy Ashdown

To build a large, motivated team of people working hard for victory requires many organisational steps but, above all, it requires emotion. Whatever mix of determination, hope and fear it is that drives people to help, unless you tug people's heartstrings, attempts at building an organisation merely constructs an empty, soulless failure.

Tony Benn, the Labour MP who notched up fifty years in Parliament including time in the Cabinet, used to tell this story in the political stump speech of his youth. Out travelling one day, he said, he met three builders working on a construction site. Wondering what was going on, he walked up to the first one and asked: 'What are you doing?' 'A lot of overtime,' joked the person back. Amused, but not enlightened, he then went up to another and asked again, 'What is it you are doing?' 'Can't you see?' he replied. 'I'm chipping stone.' Finally, Benn went up to a third and asked once more. This time the answer came: 'I'm building a cathedral.'

The cathedral builder was also doing overtime and chipping stone, yet he was also inspired by the bigger vision.

So, as a candidate, ask yourself at the outset, what is *your* vision? It will draw on many of the elements we discuss elsewhere in this book. It will doubtless draw on your own personal story. It will encompass why you are better than the other person at the job being contested. It will show why your team should travel with you on the road ahead.

You could start at the end and work backwards: what is it you want to achieve in office? Once you have a fix on that you should be able to explain where that desire comes from (often elements of your personal story) and why other people should help you to achieve it.

Your vision should be big and broad (but credible and achievable too). Then you can use it as a base for many other planks in your campaign.

It will help to underpin your campaign plan: it is essential to know where you are heading before you get into the detail of objectives, milestones and timetables.

It will inform your message to voters.

It will help to gather up and guide your campaign team. The helpers on a campaign need to see their own vision reflected in yours. It may be an intangible vision rather than a tangible one. But it also needs to translate into practical outcomes that motivate people to get involved: anything from a new police station to a revived railway line.

A big vision on its own can seem unachievable and too much to hope for. Alongside it needs to be a sense of the next few small steps someone can take to help bring it about. They do not need to know for sure what all the steps are on the long road to realising that vision, just the next few steps, made to seem small and easy. As Indira Gandhi put it, 'Break that big plan into small steps and take the first step right away.'

That way helpers know what to do next, and why it will be worthwhile. They will feel they are helping build a movement, not mere cogs in a machine.

We have quoted Paddy Ashdown and Tony Benn in this section so it seems only right to conclude with Margaret Thatcher. Whatever one's view of the former Prime Minister's politics, it is impossible to deny the consistency of her vision. Her personal story deeply influenced her politics and public persona. The homespun values of the market town corner shop were every bit as powerful a rallying cry as 'from the log cabin to the White House'.

In her own words: 'It's passionately interesting for me that the things that I learned in a small town, in a very modest home, are just the things that I believe have won the election.'

CHAPTER 25

LET PEOPLE HELP YOU

*To join in those days you had to go through several stages
of endurance to test that you were really committed.*
John O'Farrell on his experience of trying to join
the Labour Party in the mid-1980s

Given how much time many politicians and campaigners spend lamenting how there is too much to do and too few hours in the day, it is curious that so many are rather poor at letting people help them, let alone actively encouraging them to do so.

The occasional excessive optimist who thinks they can do it all themselves aside, more often this is an accidental side-effect of how they go about doing things rather than a deliberate policy of shouting 'go away' at anyone who looks mildly positive.

It is important to structure the way you do things so that it makes it easy for other people to help. That was the real lesson from Barack Obama's 2008 US presidential campaign. His use of technology may have got the headlines, but what made it so successful was a team-building, people-involving mindset right from the very top. Without that, the technology would have been lifeless code, achieving little worthy of note. He got so many people involved because getting people involved was a priority.

In the UK, during the tail end of the last Labour

government, former Deputy Prime Minister John Prescott exemplified this more inclusive campaigning approach with his attacks on bankers, their pay and (lack of) performance. He did not just attack them, he offered up many ways people could get involved in and strengthen his campaign, such as placing material in social media that people could share and running a petition. That meant people who agreed with his views had many ways they could help rather than simply read a report of what Prescott was up to, nod in agreement and then get on with whatever else they were doing.

Any campaign can achieve the same end with a simple change in mindset.

For each task in the campaign think, 'How can we do this in a way that makes it easy for more people to be involved?'

Perhaps you are planning a campaign on the run-down state of shopping high streets in your area. Pulling together some research, photographs and personal accounts to inform and enliven the campaign is a necessary early step. But do you do that solely by lining up some help at campaign HQ or do you ask people who live near the high streets to go and gather evidence to help with the campaign?

When it comes to lobbying for a policy change, do you simply have one high-end person-to-person approach or do you give your supporters ways to help – not only signing a petition you can present, but giving them information about newspapers they can write to or other politicians they can lobby (and how) in support of the campaign?

Make it easy for people to help. Don't let rigid systems deter people – if someone wants to deliver some leaflets for your campaign but only has time to deliver to her own street, do not turn her away because you only offer leaflets in bundles of 500. If you are running a petition that affects a community, why not let each person who signs the petition have fifty leaflets about the campaign to deliver near their home – it does not matter if you do not know precisely which doors they have gone to.

Sometimes it requires a little relaxation in control – after all, who knows quite what a supporter of yours will say in a meeting and what they will say to a neighbour? It also requires having a range of different tasks so that people with different interests and abilities can help in the ways that suit them.

More fundamentally, it requires the right outlook. Do not treat supporters as passive spectators but as people who can become active participants in the campaign, helping it to grow and achieve more of its goals.

CHAPTER 26

ASK NICELY, ASK OFTEN, ASK WELL

A boy was struggling to lift a heavy stone when his
father called out to him: 'Are you using all your strength?'
'Yes, I am,' the child said impatiently. 'No, you are not,'
replied the father. 'For I am right here just waiting, and
you haven't asked me to help you.' Anonymous

So, you need a team and you know you need to lead it. How, then, do you get people to join the team and do things? By asking, and by asking well.

Human beings are often remarkably reluctant to ask others for help, afraid of receiving a 'no' – or a ruder response. But if you don't ask, you don't get. Indeed, we would go further: you need to ask regularly or you risk people drifting away.

Ed got involved with a single-issue pressure group a few years back. It was campaigning against a move to change the law on an issue he felt strongly about. He heard their spokesperson on the radio and signed up as a supporter via their website. There was an initial contact with a simple campaign ask, an update or two and then silence. The legislative initiative had been defeated but the issue remained. Three years later the issue burst to life again. An email arrived (to an email address that had been retired for months). Then silence once more. Your campaigning author did not bother to get involved again.

This is a simple story but one that is almost sure to be too common to people who get involved with political parties. They make contact in a burst of enthusiasm (we hear many stories of the hardships people endure even finding someone in their community to make contact with!). Then there is silence. Investigate further and often you will find well-meaning (overstretched) activists who 'planned to get in touch but didn't like to bother them'. You need to meet enthusiasm with enthusiasm and to give volunteers a sense of a dynamic organisation that is determined to achieve its goals. Keeping in touch and asking for help regularly is a key part of that.

When asking for help, remember to ask nicely – often you are asking people to give up their own time voluntarily so that you can win political power. They need to like you in order to be happy with that exchange! That is not only a matter of good manners and polite vocabulary; it is also a matter of giving people proper attention when asking for help. Even if your approach is not face-to-face, people can still tell the difference between an off-hand, quick email, phone call or letter asking for help and one that has some care and attention given to it.

And ask often. Even if someone has declined to help once, it does not mean you should never ask them again. A different question at a different time can still get a yes. Even the same question may also get a yes second time round. Make the most of the opportunities you have: Mark has an obsession about sign-in sheets for meetings and rallies, for example.

Always have one – and make sure there is one on every chair – and always give people the chance to offer help by ticking a box on the sheet.

Think about the nature of the opportunity, too. UK politician Ed Davey pioneered asking friends and family who are not politically active to help with his election campaign on its final weekend. The urgency and specific nature of the request makes it something people are willing to respond to, even if they normally have no interest in politics.

When asking, you need to frame the question well, make it clear what you are asking for, why you are asking, how it can be done and when it needs doing. The easier it is for someone to envisage themselves carrying out the task, the more likely they are to say yes. That also means it is best to ask for something that is only a small step up from what they currently are doing – or a small, concrete and finite task if they are not yet doing anything.

Above all, just ask.

CHAPTER 27

MAKE THE JOBS FIT THE PEOPLE

He led, he did not drive. G. Vibert Douglas on
Sir Ernest Shackleton

Ernest Shackleton led his crew through two years of survival on an ice shelf when their ship became stuck in 1915. His leadership skills are widely praised as exceptional and, while you cannot seriously compare an election campaign to a life-and-death endurance struggle in the Antarctic, many of the lessons about leading a team are universal.

Part of his skill was in ensuring that all the members of the team had meaningful and challenging work to do that matched their abilities. At the root of his capacity to do that was a willingness to relate to team members as individuals, to communicate with them, and to break down established cliques and processes. The need to survive bound the members of Shackleton's expedition together. Campaign volunteers can walk away and do other things with their time, so an effective team leader should work especially hard at keeping the team motivated and working well.

One of our favourite campaigners broke many of the rules in this book. He was extraordinarily single-minded about the task of winning. He achieved an enormous amount through sheer force of energy. But he was almost unique and he almost lost. His team of supporters were dedicated and hard-working, too, but they were often in the wrong jobs, pushed into tackling the next most urgent task regardless of their skills or interests. The list of urgent tasks was always growing because the volunteers burned out or drifted away. Taking time to match the skills of your team to the tasks at hand can pay major dividends in the effectiveness of your campaign.

We talk a lot in this book about the importance of prioritising, and trying to complete the most important task first is usually a very good rule. However, when it comes to team building it is a rule that you should bend from time to time – and even sometimes break completely.

That is because building a team of volunteers requires balancing both what you need them to do and what people want to do. The same applies with employed staff – perhaps less so, because staff can (within limits) be given instructions and should be recruited with the skills in mind to tackle the most important jobs. With volunteers in particular, asking them to do tasks they like or value is preferable over asking them to do what you really need done most – as long as it is a deliberate part of a plan to get more people involved and doing more.

We are not going to give you a list of job titles for the team. One of the key lessons we try to stress is about flexibility and we are aware that readers will be leading campaigns that vary hugely in size. A generic list of tasks would not help you much. One exception we will make, though, is to stress that volunteers need managers so you need to find someone (or more than one) to take on the role of volunteer manager.

You also need to identify what needs doing and to work out what resources are needed to complete the tasks by the required deadline. That will tell you how many people you need in your team. It will also help you decide which tasks need a group of people doing them, which means you need managers as well as 'doers'.

The best way to get someone started as a helper is to get them to do something that is easy, convenient and interesting for them. Invest time in talking and listening to them. They will need to learn how to do their task and how it fits into the campaign as a whole. They might be able to suggest a way to do the task better.

Give volunteers the kind of induction that businesses often offer to new staff. Offer them training, introduce them to other parts of the campaign and ask if they would like to be involved. Encourage them to ask questions and introduce them to other people in the campaign, especially ones they are likely to find a common interest with.

You will need to recognise that this means investing resources in building and maintaining your volunteer team. It is often something local campaigns do very poorly because they can become dominated by groups of insiders who are not very welcoming to new people. Find a volunteer co-ordinator with strong people skills and give them the brief of developing and motivating your team: the returns will be measurable.

Be imaginative in your approach, too. Ed, working on a mayoral contest in one of Europe's newest democracies, came across teams of students campaigning on bicycles in the downtown area of the capital. Kitted out with matching sweatshirts, they were eye-catching and enthusiastic as they handed out fliers and chatted to voters. A few years later, in the same city, all the parties had invested in small gazebos pitched alongside the streets. They each contained two or three dejected-looking students who sat and talked to each other as voters passed by barely noticing the campaign. Imagination and freshness are important virtues in getting the most out of your campaign – and out of your volunteers.

So the way to getting a big volunteer team is a variation on the old adage of not trying to fit square pegs in round holes. If you have square pegs, come up with square holes for them to fill – and if you have round pegs, rustle up some round holes.

CHAPTER 28

GET THE LEGAL
DETAILS RIGHT

The best candidates are on the ballot and out of jail.

There is a harsh simplicity about the ballot paper at election time: you are either on it or not.

That harsh simplicity left sixty candidates in the London Borough of Harrow unable to stand in 2002 after the legal paperwork for the elections was not completed correctly. Several of those candidates were incumbents who thus found themselves out of office before the campaign had even started.

Even if you do stand, failures to get legal details right can still cost you your seat – e.g. if it is discovered you are not qualified after all, or if failure to keep to election and finance law causes a scandal that forces resignation.

The media and the public quite rightly usually take a hard-line view: if you think you are fit to set the rules that other people have to follow, you should be able to understand and follow rules yourself. Only occasionally is a more charitable view taken, such as in the case of the Welsh Assembly member who ran into trouble over whether he was qualified to stand for election in 2011 but won cross-party and public support because the guidance he was sent by the official Electoral Commission turned out to have been wrong.

In the UK, the forms used in public elections were designed decades ago. Even though UK electoral law has been regularly revised in recent years, the language on the paperwork can seem impenetrable to the untrained eye. The law changes regularly and there are dangers lurking in the arcane corners of the legislation.

Usually a candidate appoints a representative – an 'election agent' – to oversee compliance with the legal and administrative aspects of the campaign. A candidate must be sure that the person appointed as agent is capable (fully understands the law) and willing to do the job carefully, accurately and well. A candidate should take the time to get to know the agent and find out about their experience and skills. Make sure they have access to good quality advice and, when needed, training.

There are usually three sources of legal advice and guidance available to candidates: from their own party, from local election officials and from the central election administrator. The advice provided by a party to its own candidates is, at least as far as the main parties go, usually of a high quality and often mixes in legal requirements with good practice. Advice from election officials can be, in the UK, remarkably varied. Both of the authors have experience of trying to sort out problems where an official has provided old forms, incomplete advice or an opinion that is not based accurately on the law.

If you believe that the official advice you have been given is wrong, get it checked by someone who knows the details of the law.

As with any case of delegation, once they appoint an agent a good candidate will let them get on with the job – remember this is not the same as then ignoring the role and blindly hoping the job is done well. Even the best of agents make mistakes and have moments of crisis that cloud their judgement. And even if it is clearly an agent's mistake that causes a problem with the law, the media and the public often – understandably – point the finger of blame at the candidate.

A good candidate, therefore, takes care of their agent and takes care of their own reputation – and that means they take care to check that the law is being followed.

CHAPTER 29

SAY THANK YOU

I feel a strange sensation. If it is not indigestion,
it must be gratitude. Benjamin Disraeli

Politics (and society) has come a long way since
the days of Disraeli. We appreciate the Victorian
Prime Minister's acid wit but it would not get him
very far in building a modern campaign.

George Bush Senior, by contrast, is not known for
his wit but he was very effective at building support
for his candidacy. His political career has been rather
overshadowed by being succeeded (and defeated) by
one of the most charismatic and controversial politicians of modern American history, Bill Clinton, and
by his son also becoming President and exceeding
even Clinton in the controversy he generated.

Nevertheless, it was an impressive career: the
youngest aviator in the US Navy during the Second
World War, a congressman, Ambassador to the
United Nations, Director of the CIA, Vice President
for eight years and then President of the USA for a
further four years.

Part of the secret of his success was his directness
– including telling Nixon to his face at a Cabinet
meeting that he should resign over Watergate.

Another part of his success was his willingness to
say 'thank you'. He had a strongly ingrained habit

of writing thank-you notes. It certainly made him a stronger candidate and even a man as powerful as the President of the United States of America frequently benefits from having a reservoir of personal goodwill to tap.

Saying thank you is, of course, nothing new, because saying thank you has great power. As Oscar Wilde put it, 'The smallest act of kindness is worth more than the grandest intention.'

A successful team is one in which all the members of the team feel they have a strong stake in reaching its goal. Candidates often have a strong personality – the job does not tend to attract wallflowers. A good candidate will make use of their personality to motivate team members. One of our favourite candidates regularly drove professional campaigners to distraction. She was hyperactive and disorganised, but she was also fantastically good at connecting with people on an individual level. Saying thank you was second nature to her but it was all the more powerful because she expressed her gratitude with genuine enthusiasm. As President Kennedy said, 'As we express our gratitude, we must never forget that the highest appreciation is not to utter words, but to live by them.'

All of this is so important because campaigns rely on volunteers for their success (and by the way, do not forget to thank their families too). When training activists there was a serious message behind our regular joking reference to the candidate as nothing more than 'the legal necessity' in the campaign. Most political campaigns rely on the work of volunteers and successful campaigns recognise their central importance. By their nature, of course, volunteers are not paid for the work they do. Making sure you say thank you is one way of rewarding them for their efforts. Saying it often and making clear that you mean it is important, too.

Modern mass communications techniques have become ubiquitous and increasingly sophisticated. That makes it easy to *say* thank you to lots of people with relatively little effort. But as with so much else in life, the effort put in is generally linked closely to the credit gained. One candidate we know invested a huge amount of time and effort adding a personal PS to mass-produced thank-you letters in his campaign. That personal touch won him many friends (and a reprimand from his bank when his signature changed so much they no longer accepted his cheques!).

In the hurly-burly of a campaign, it is easy to let good intentions slip, but remember, if a candidate wins they get a job, power and (even now) prestige. For most helpers, all they come away with is the pleasure of seeing the candidate get all three. Saying thank you is the very least a candidate can do – this way their helpers are likely to help in the re-election campaign too!

CHAPTER 30

DEALING WITH
DIFFICULT PEOPLE

*When dealing with people, remember you are not deal-
ing with creatures of logic, but with creatures of emotion.*
Dale Carnegie

There is one thing worse than dealing with difficult people: ignoring difficult people. Problems
with difficult people do not magically disappear or
sort themselves out and ignoring just delays – and
often worsens – the inevitable. How, then, do you deal
with difficult people well?

If step one is deciding not to ignore the problem,
step two is to keep calm and be polite (sometimes
much easier said than done, of course). Make time to
prepare for the conversation. Mentally, so you do not
have steam coming out of your ears, but also literally:
making notes of what you want to say will help you
focus and should give you a better understanding of
the reasons for the problem.

Then, listen. Letting the other person do the talking and asking them questions to prompt for more
information will stop the conversation becoming a
confrontation and it will help you understand what
the reasons behind the problem are. 'Open' questions
are best – that is, those which do not lend themselves
to simple, short answers such as 'no', 'yesterday' or

'chocolate', but instead open up the conversation by requiring longer answers.

During the conversation, try to understand the other person's perspective, particularly any fears, insecurities or missing information that may be causing their behaviour. This will help you to understand the reasons that lie behind the problem.

Are you spotting a pattern here? Most times, problems are caused not by people who woke up that morning and said 'today I am going to make the candidate's life difficult'. Most of the time they are caused by a failure of communication. That does not always mean a problem can be solved in a nice warm fluffy way that leaves everyone happy. Sometimes, when a person does grasp why you need them to do a task in a particular way, they are still not prepared to do it. In this instance, it is better to take the task away from them or even to part company all together. This is a conclusion that you should only reach rarely, but sometimes it is the right conclusion. Remember it is not just about you and your needs or them and theirs, but also about the team.

In our experience, most often problems can be dealt with by talking them through (note the emphasis on talking – dealing with people by email can have disastrous results).

Bear in mind that in the heat of the moment, people often say things which either they do not literally believe are true – or if they do, they no longer do so once they have calmed down. Do not get too caught up in any particularly outrageous things you may hear. Instead, focus on common ground and follow up on any hints about what can be done to deal with long-running annoyances. That may seem very small scale, but the task is to work out practical steps forward – and also to deal with the difficult behaviour, not miraculously to transform the person into a saint.

You then need to build trust by starting to find solutions or ways of improving matters. Often the difficult person will be very receptive to being asked about such steps – and frustrated that no one asked them such a question previously!

It can help if you can identify what motivates them – it is no good telling them that their actions are upsetting to you if they could not care less about your feelings.

It is important to be clear with them about the problem (and hopefully the solution). It is natural to want to avoid confrontation but do not lose clarity – that will only mean the problem persists or gets worse. Sometimes you will need to remove someone, a difficult decision but it will be worth it in the long run if you judge they are taking more from the campaign than they are adding.

Our final tip is this. We can guarantee that you will have to deal with difficult people during the campaign. So use that knowledge and plan for it. Talk to your team about their experiences, learn from them and develop your own skills. They are sure to come in useful.

CHAPTER 31

WHY PEOPLE FAIL
TO BUILD TEAMS

No, it is not quicker to do things yourself.

Flick through the business and self-improvement books in your local bookshop and you will find advice aplenty on team building. There are so many books not because the authors are unimaginative; rather team building is important, is hugely beneficial and is often tricky to get right. We know of several people whose first instinct is always to tackle a task themselves. Often they can achieve success in the short term but, equally often, they fail in the longer term once they have reached the limits of their own capacity.

People can find many reasons not to build a team: it's easier that way, everyone else will be worse than me, I will lose control, it takes lots of effort to begin with. Winning candidates can look past all of these and see why it is good to build teams.

There are three basic reasons why building a team makes sense for a political campaign. First, and most obviously, it is almost impossible to do everything yourself and win. Reaching enough voters with your message and persuading them to vote for you is a huge challenge, as you will already have gathered.

The second reason why teams matter is because

political campaigns are complex as well as big. They demand a wide range of different skills. Your campaign will work best if you identify those key skills (tip: read this book to help you do that) and build a team that brings together those skills in an effective way.

The third reason is simply to reassure your supporters that they are not alone. A big team will give off a buzz, it will be noticed and it will lead to other people asking why they themselves are not involved. It will gain a momentum all of its own.

Perhaps the biggest obstacle to team building in the political context is the temptation to think 'it's quicker to do it myself'. With volunteers that very often is the case – training people, motivating them, having some drop out as not quite able or willing, thanking them, recruiting, all takes time. It is tempting – but wrong – to think 'I will just do it myself – that will be quicker and I will know the job is done'.

Hence the big reason why team building fails is that it never really starts.

The next most common reason in our experience is that team building requires leadership: you need to not only send out requests for help but also actively seek out team members and cultivate them.

We have talked about effective ways to lead a team. Towards the end of the book we also talk about the need for a candidate to maintain a healthy work–life balance. An important part of building an effective team is paying attention to the people in a team and ensuring they maintain a sensible balance in their lives too. Do not let people (either volunteers or staff) burn themselves out in the heat of the campaign: it is bad for them, for the campaign (mistakes start to happen) and for the team. And do not discourage people from combining the campaign with spending time on other things. It will help to keep them engaged and motivated.

For a team to work it needs to have a sense of purpose, direction and progress – all of which requires regular communication and consultation, the absence of which also often causes political campaign teams to fail.

THE RESOURCES

If what you did yesterday still looks big to you, you haven't done enough today. Mikhail Gorbachev

Building a team means building up your most important resource – a pool of talented, committed helpers. Yet even the best of helpers need resources to be effective. In Part 3 we look at how to acquire and organise resources. In an election campaign there is no substitute for hard work but you will also need to work smart to win.

CHAPTER 32

CAMPAIGN PLANNING

Luck is the crossroads where preparation and
opportunity meet. Anonymous

For some tasks, making it up as you go along can work. That is if what you are doing is simple, has little in the way of inter-dependent steps and does not involve making use of other people's help and resources at the right time and in the right way. Winning an election fails all those tests, which is why election campaigns fail without proper planning.

Plans can vary hugely in size and complexity depending on how far away polling day is and how many voters are involved, but all good plans provide a clear overall map for what the key activities and deadlines are, and as a result what resources will be needed at what point of the campaign.

A good plan helps avoid two common logistical problems: bottlenecks holding up a campaign and help being wasted because you are not ready to use it.

Some bottlenecks are inevitable. Knowing when they are likely to occur, however, allows the key people involved to plan their time to minimise them. The bottleneck then becomes just another step in the campaign rather than the cause of long delays.

Making full use of the potential help available also requires good planning. Keep volunteers busy. If you are a couple of days late with the next campaign leaflet, for example, volunteer deliverers might go unused. You cannot get back that lost volunteer time, which is why a good plan guides a campaign around such mistakes.

A major part of elections in the UK is the Royal Mail's 'Freepost', which delivers some of the campaign literature for candidates free of charge. It is a great place to look if you need to test the importance of planning. The Royal Mail manage a massive logistics operation to make millions of deliveries across the country every day. They have an extensive set of rules for the Freepost operation to make sure they do not break the law (content and format of the leaflet for example) and to make sure they are able to fit your mailing into their delivery schedule before polling day. They also employ a large number of people. You do not, and the preparation involved in planning producing, printing and packing 60,000 mailings, then delivering them to the depot by the deadline, is enormous.

Get the Freepost planning wrong and you miss an opportunity to get your message across to voters. In every election we see reports of Freepost disasters – sometimes they make it to the press such as when a candidate's message was delivered in Latin because someone had failed to remove the placeholder text used by printers when they were waiting for the real text to arrive. Usually the problems arise because of a failure to plan properly and to make time to check and re-check details.

A good start for a campaign plan is a simple diary structure, with the key dates (e.g. deadline for legal registration, deadline for nomination papers, polling day and so on) and the key campaign activities (e.g. deliver first general leaflet). Then next to each of those activities list the resources, people and preparatory steps required, using those to fill in further dates in the plan (e.g., first general leaflet requires photographs, so put in deadline for taking photographs).

Make sure everyone knows what their key tasks are. Make it clear, too, who is taking the lead in managing those tasks so that someone is responsible for chasing up actions. Figure out the most practical way for team members to meet together. It may be necessary to meet 'online' rather than in person but the meetings need to be regular and focused.

Plans will evolve but once you have the basic framework, share it with the key team and make sure everyone looks at it regularly so they know what needs to be done before it is too late.

CHAPTER 33

CAMPAIGN BUDGETS

*A campaign budget is about winning,
not making a profit.*

If this book were a motivational masterpiece, it
would tell the reader to embrace the liberating
power of budgets. It would tell you that financial planning is a crucial step on the path to political Nirvana.
In truth, most campaigns live in something close to
a state of purgatory. And any campaign manager will
tell you that there is no sense of liberation until the
books are closed – long after the cheering crowds have
left and the candidate has set out on her new career.

Anyone planning an election campaign does have
one big thing going for them: the target is piercingly
clear. Get more votes than the other candidate on
election day.

That is one big piece of knowledge to help shape
your planning. Sadly, there the clarity often ends. Two
big unknowns in particular cloud the horizon: how
much do you *need* to spend and how much will your
opponent spend?

No one has written the definitive formula to tell
us how much it costs to get someone to vote for you.
In the 2008 US presidential election, the two leading
Democrat candidates spent $200 million each, just to
be selected as their party's candidate. And they fought
each other to a virtual draw. On the flip side, party

yalty and moribund opposition organisations mean that many British MPs can be sure of re-election time after time while spending almost nothing on their campaigns.

It is a fair bet that spending more than your opponent will increase your chances of winning. But it will not guarantee it and your opponent is not obliged to tell you in advance how much they plan to spend. You have to get smart about your campaign: you have to plan your route to success knowing that the map only takes you part way there.

You will notice that up to now we have not mentioned *raising* money, just spending it. That brings us, airport book style, to the One Critical Thing To Know about election campaign budgeting: you have to let your objective (winning the election) drive your budgets and fundraising.

Far too many candidates start off with very few funds, don't like the idea of raising money or asking people for donations and so draw up a cautious, insipid budget that nominally is about winning but really is about sinking into comfortable defeat.

It is important to keep proper control over your campaign fund. There is a good legal reason for this: you will need to file returns of your campaign spend once it is over. There are sound ethical reasons for doing it: you should be accountable to the people who fund your campaign and to voters for what you do with the money. There are common sense budgetary reasons for doing it: you are more likely to spend the money wisely if you keep a close eye on where it goes, therefore minimising waste and maximising impact.

If you are launching a winning campaign with colleagues who are used to losing, you will have to take them with you. Some of them will resist. That is why you have to be absolutely clear that your budget is driven by your objective: winning. And winning will be for them as much as it is for you.

Make sure your figures are credible. Do not over-estimate or under-estimate: both will leave you open to challenge. Do not overlook mundane costs that can mount up. Any house makeover programme will show you how many ambitious projects are undone by forgotten overheads and over-optimistic pricing.

And then, once your plan and your budget are set you can begin to work out how to raise the funds to pay for them.

CHAPTER 34

DATA IS YOUR
ORGANISATIONAL LIFEBLOOD

Errors using inadequate data are much less than those using no data at all. Charles Babbage

Data makes your campaign efficient because it means you can reach the right people with your messages. Political campaigners have understood the importance of data for longer than you might think.

Look back through the records of UK political parties from a hundred years ago and you will find something that might surprise you. One of the main electioneering tasks – one that warranted the employment of party agents to make sure it happened – was the annual registration drive. For the registration drive to work effectively the local party needed comprehensive and up-to-date records. Data mattered then in electioneering and it still matters now.

Ask yourself what you need to do to win. Encourage your supporters to vote? Ask helpers for a little bit more help? Send a rebuttal email about a breaking news story? Let parents know about a new schools policy? You need data for all of that.

Data is what tells you who the most important voters are to contact in the next week. Data tells you which messages will work best with those people.

Data tells you who is willing to help contact those voters. Data tells you how to get hold of them.

A very simple example of the power of data came from the Dunfermline by-election, the scene of a shock victory by the Liberal Democrats as the party nationally was plunged into a leadership crisis.

The party had very little voter ID data for the constituency, which meant the most valuable task was the phone calls made before polling day. The initial canvass data was inspected, matched to geographic and demographic information, and a target list was created of priority people to call whose characteristics most closely matched identified supporters. The list was then tested by phoning voters at random and it was consistently found that calling the priority list resulted in half as many supporters again being identified for each batch of calls than calling at random. Increasing the campaign's hit rate by 50 per cent was a major productivity boost.

To be able to identify your own similar lessons, you need to love and cherish data, and keep a close eye on both quality and quantity. Far too often campaigners fail to keep an eye on either, resulting in lost opportunities and mistakes made.

Identify the key pieces of data you need, for example supporters willing to put up posters and voters pledged to vote for you. Then make sure someone is regularly tallying and reporting the totals so the campaign knows how its data gathering is going. (Regularly checking the totals also gives an immediate warning if a horrible data mistake has been made and records lost, over-written or misfiled – something that happens far too often for comfort.)

But also make sure the campaign team is checking on the quality of the data. For each of the key pieces of data, think of one way of checking if the data is good and make sure you keep track of this, too, e.g. what proportion of the poster sites called on during the last week said yes to a poster?

That way you can be sure your campaign is getting the high-quality data it needs or, if not, you will know in good time that you have a problem and can fix it.

CHAPTER 35

BUILDING DATA IS A LONG-TERM BUSINESS

Data is what distinguishes the dilettante from the artist. George V. Higgins

If you are very lucky, a huge volume of data will flow into your campaign very quickly. Perhaps a petition will really take off and hundreds of signatures come in the post every day. But most of the time, data is the tortoise of the childhood fable, not the hare. It is such a big task that you cannot hope to do it in one short, fast rush. Gradual, persistent accumulation of data wins the day over thinking that all it takes is a sudden burst of activity as polling day nears.

The reason is simple: most data degrades only slowly over time, remaining far better than having no data at all. A list of supporters from last year's election will not be 100 per cent right for this year's election – people move, die and change opinions – but usually it will be far better than having nothing.

Similarly, lists of email addresses for voters degrade over time as people move, die or change their email address (especially if the one you have for them is a work-based address). Typically, in the UK email lists decay at the rate of less than 1 per cent per month. That certainly means you cannot just put together an email list and then forget about adding to or correcting it ever again. However, it explains why, at general election time, candidates we have worked with typically use 80 per cent of email lists gathered in the previous year.

Or to put it the other way round, by accumulating data steadily over time, these campaigns have email lists five times bigger than if they just started in the year running up to an election.

Accumulating data over time also means accumulating data over different sorts of elections, across which there will be a range of different candidates. Working closely and collaboratively over those elections, therefore, is very important. If the data is gathered in the name of a political party, it is fairly straightforward to keep to the law and also share the data with all the different candidates standing in the party's name.

In the United States, parties have grown experienced in building up shared data sets year after year rather than each candidate keeping the data to themselves.

Accumulating data over time means you need to be extra careful about making backups and checking the data is correct, as the longer you accumulate data, the higher the chances of something going wrong at some point. (See Chapter 41 for more on this.)

A good approach to take therefore is to work out how much data you need at key points in the future and work backwards to see what that means for each month in the interim – and then plan your data gathering accordingly. Do you need to be gathering an average of five email addresses a week or fifty or 500 for the next year? Know the answer to that and you can then plan your activities accordingly, to the right scale.

CHAPTER 36

WAYS OF GETTING DATA

Gathering data isn't just for geeks.

Given the importance of data and the need to collect large amounts of high-quality data, it is important that data gathering is seen as everyone's job and that they all understand that data can be found in a variety of places. Avoid the temptation to centralise data collection because people who are out and about in their neighbourhoods and communities can always gather more.

Typically, in mediocre campaigns, gathered data is passed on to someone who types it into a computer and most people never hear of it again. Sometimes someone deliberately hoards the data to protect 'my data' about 'my area' – protected, we assume, from the hidden evils of someone doing something useful with it for a wider benefit.

That one-way, semi-mystical process means people do not build up a shared understanding of the importance of data and the reward of feeling a sense of progress with data. The result? Most people end up not really bothered about doing their bit to help.

That is a mistake because everyone in the team can and should gather data in their own ways. You need to have a shared understanding of its importance and that comes in part from good communication:

explaining the importance, communicating progress and thanking people for their efforts.

One simple example is the local newspaper. These are full of useful information about your campaign. Marriage and death notices mean that you can update your records without having to wait for the official changes – that can avoid embarrassment or hurt. In one parliamentary by-election, the combination of a long campaign and an elderly electorate meant that updating records with local death notices was not simply a useful tip, it became essential to avoid offending large numbers of relatives. Information on who is involved in which local organisation, who has backed what campaign and even who is a regular writer of letters to the newspapers all helps fill out your data.

You can also identify non-political information such as who can be congratulated for winning a flower show or receiving an award. Even in this cynical age, a note of congratulations is often hugely appreciated – especially if it is from an incumbent politician. Caring about your community – and being seen to care – can make a real difference to your campaign.

Of course, some aspects of data are very confidential and should not be shared around widely, both for reasons of competitive advantage (you do not want your opponents to know exactly how you are doing) and for reasons of personal privacy (some information is rightly private).

However, that should not be a reason to keep everything secret. It may be as simple as regularly letting the team know how many new people were talked to in the last month or how many new helpers were identified – a few headline figures help give people a sense of progress. Add to that the occasional thank-you prize for someone who has done particularly well at collecting data and you can quickly build up the right sort of culture.

Two sources of data are often under-used. First, what members of the campaign already know. Whether it is mobile phone numbers for local helpers, knowledge of who the key people are in local organisations in the area or information about who put up posters at a previous election, there is often a large amount of knowledge floating around in people's heads or their own address books, spreadsheets and scraps of paper. Collating as much of this as possible into the campaign's official records is an easy and effective way of boosting data collection.

Second, 'internal' events are a great source of information. Have a sign-in sheet at your events which gathers people's names, email addresses and phone numbers, and you will rapidly accumulate very useful contact information. Even if the event is a local party meeting with only paid-up members present, there are almost always pieces of information you get from the sign-in sheets that are not yet in the campaign or party's official records.

Both of these come with a bonus in addition to the data the campaign team members themselves bring in: they help set that campaign-wide culture that data matters and everyone can do their bit.

CHAPTER 37

MAKING USE OF
DEMOGRAPHIC DATA

Fill in the gaps in your own data with other people's data.

One of the authors has neighbours above, next door and opposite. Across these four household, three have young children and one does not. Three are private sector accommodation and one is a council flat. Three contain at least one driver and one does not.

Despite these differences, the households do share some important similarities. If you are deciding what issues to write to these people about, you can make a reasonable calculation of which ones to pick. Local education policy, for example, or traffic congestion will hit the mark with most of the residents. If you write to all four households about such issues, not everyone will find them of interest but you will have pretty good odds.

That sort of picture of households is what campaigns and political parties can buy from firms such as Experian with its MOSAIC classification scheme, based on information from sources such as the census. You do not know for sure the attributes of a particular person (and rightly so, given much of the data is from anonymous sources), but putting together lots of data from different sources gives a good picture of the area.

In many ways this information is a more advanced form of the modelling that you can carry out using your own data (see Chapter 38).

Such data can be very valuable, as long as you have realistic expectations of what it can add to your campaign. Because of its potential value to businesses it is getting more detailed all the time but we are not quite yet living in the film *Minority Report* – we can all think of poorly targeted advertising that we have received in the mail. (As a long-time vegetarian, Mark finds the regular adverts for meat directed at him a good reminder of how poorly data is often used and how misdirected messages result.)

Remember the example at the start of this section – walk up to any of those households and you may be disappointed (one in four, in fact) if you expect to be sure to find children in it. Across all of them, however, there is a much higher chance that people in this group will be interested in the state of schools than if you randomly picked homes to target.

Another useful source of data is from opinion polls. Even if your campaign is not able to afford any of its own, national opinion polls often have much data that is of use. This might include, for example, how support for parties varies across gender and age groups or which issues voters view as most important.

The headline figures reported in the media rarely go much beyond which party or candidate is most popular. The full data tables, which in some countries – such as the UK – most pollsters make readily available via their website or if you ask, are another matter. When you start looking at them, you will also find that often media outlets commission polls with many questions and do not publish them all – especially if the answers run counter to their own editorial line! They have paid for the work, and if you can use their questions even if they have not, then that is all to the good for your campaign.

It is important to use this data intelligently, though. Even if the aggregate figures from a poll suggest that an issue is very important you need to judge whether it is the right one for you to campaign on. Is it a 'hot button' issue that will fade from memory by the time election day comes along? Is it an issue that appeals to a section of the electorate who are set in their voting habits and will not vote for you even if you explain your position on it? Handle this data with intelligence and care, but above all, handle it. Otherwise you will be letting valuable data aid your opponent but not yourself.

CHAPTER 38

MODELLING AND POOLS

*An experienced campaign runs itself backwards. That is,
it determines how many votes it needs to win and builds
a plan back from election day to get that many votes.*
Steve Pearson and Ford O'Connell

Sometimes there just is not enough data to feed all your needs. In an ideal world, you might know the likely voting intention of every possible elector. In the real world, modelling comes in to help; it is a way of filling in the gaps.

The simplest form is by looking at your data on people's voting intentions and matching it up against people's gender and where they live to see if there is a pattern in how support varies. Are men in one part of the electorate particularly likely to be opponents or women in another area particularly likely to be supporters? If there is a pattern, use it to estimate what the likely preferences are of people whose voting intentions you do not know. Those estimates are not the same as certain knowledge but, if they are good enough, they are better than knowing nothing.

More sophisticated analysis, often using advanced maths, looks at a wider range of factors and comes up with models that conclude that a person is x per cent likely to be a supporter, based on all the different things you know about them. As more information comes in, the model is regularly refined and improved, and the estimates for individual people also improve as more is found out about them, such as whether or not they respond to requests to sign petitions.

When doing this, make sure you use someone whose knowledge of statistics extends as far as, and further than, correlations, confidence intervals and standard deviations. Otherwise, you risk low-quality analysis picking up false patterns that lead you and your campaign astray.

In the late 1990s, Mark developed for the UK Liberal Democrats a concept called 'the pool', which is similar to the 'mailing universe' used in US politics and direct marketing. The pool was filled with the people he thought would be most likely to support the party. It contained enough people – in fact more than enough – for the party's candidate to reach the likely winning post in the election. Driven by the need to have as much information as early in the campaign as possible, the pool helped them to identify the people they should prioritise in their campaigning. It helped them to show just how far and how fast they would need to grow in order to meet their target. It also helped them to decide how to get the right messages to the right people by seeing which groups of people filled the pool and the characteristics they shared.

In the pool, a good margin has to be allowed for error and turnout – there is no point going after fewer votes than necessary to win! That may sound obvious, but it is a common mistake – targeting people you know are supporters and forgetting to compare that total with the number of voters needed to win. (See Chapter 39 for more on how to identify the priority voters.)

Prioritise the people in the pool when canvassing, whether on foot or on phone, and confirm if they are supporters or not. The model and the pool improves, with some topping up or even changes to the model necessary if too many turn out not to be supporters. The pool also provides the group of people to contact when blanket communications are not practical or affordable, for example concentrating posted direct mail on the pool.

CHAPTER 39

DECIDING WHO TO PRIORITISE

If everything is a priority, nothing is a priority.

When elected, you will represent all of the people who live in your electoral district. To get elected, though, you need to prioritise.

When confirming who the priority voters are, there are three factors to bear in mind:

- how likely they are to vote,
- how likely they are to vote for you, and
- the need not to ignore everyone else.

Predicting the behaviour of voters can be tricky, though, as the experience of one returning officer a few years ago demonstrated. Short of a suitable venue in a rural area, the returning officer ended up using the front room of a local family's large home for the polling station. A few hours after polling had started, he decided to give the polling station a call, to check with his staff that the new venue was successful. He was told that nobody had voted yet. What, not even the family in whose home the polling station was located? No, not even them – they had been and gone, deciding they were too busy to vote.

Despite this failure of a quite literal taking of the ballot box into someone's home, the ease with which someone can vote is usually a good predictor of their likeliness to vote.

Records are usually available after an election showing who voted in it. Accumulating these records over time provides an essential start to predicting if someone is likely to be a voter or a non-voter. Habits can change, but the historic pattern makes for a strong predictor.

Add this information to whether someone has a postal or proxy vote, and if they live close to a polling station, and you can start to classify people into very unlikely to vote, very likely to vote and so on. For a little more refinement, add in other demographic data, which you can compare with the many sources of national analysis about who does and does not vote.

Just to return to the question of habits for a moment, it is worth noting that important things can be learned from different sorts of elections. Turnout in national elections is generally higher than in local elections so if you only have data for a parliamentary election it may not be that good at predicting who will vote in a local election. However, if someone habitually does not vote at the high-turnout election, it is a reasonable bet they will not in the local poll either. Equally, someone who always votes in local elections is likely to turn out for the general election. Keep watch, too, for your supporters who suddenly stop voting. If a large number do so, you may wish to ask them why.

For the question of whether or not someone is likely to vote for you, the gold-standard source of information is that gathered directly from them in the current campaign. That too can be supplemented from other sources, in particular historic information about their voting preferences and whether or not they have responded to other aspects of the campaign; for example, in the absence of any other information knowing that they have signed up to your email list is a useful indicator. Again, use demographic information to enhance further the predictions, especially when there is opinion poll data that gives some appropriate leads.

However good your predictions turn out to be, do not ignore those they leave out. The predictions, after all, are never perfect – they are simply a guide to the best way to prioritise. A wider point of principle in a mass democracy is to offer yourself to any voter who might be interested. They may decide to turn their back on you, but it should be their choice and that way round.

CHAPTER 40

DO THE MATHEMATICS

Numbers rule the universe. Pythagoras

Sometimes the greatest puzzle is how to take the opposition's campaign plan seriously.

A very dangerous mistake to make is to underestimate your opponent, especially by lapsing into the comfortable thought that you are smarter than they are. In one successful campaign, the question kept on popping up: how could our opponents (the Labour Party) possibly think their campaign plan was a winning one?

Superficially it sounded plausible: hold a Labour seat by piling up the votes in the most supportive neighbourhoods. Its flaw became apparent, however, the moment you started doing the sums.

Those neighbourhoods dominated only 30 per cent of the wards; moreover, those wards were slightly smaller than the other wards with a lower turnout than the other 70 per cent. No matter how big the Labour win in those 30 per cent, it just was not possible to win across the district. What's more, the Liberal Democrat strategy (win by a small margin across the other 70 per cent and not get smashed out of sight in the 30 per cent) not only extrapolated to a victory when the sums were done, it also had the bonus that the hardest part (winning the 70 per cent) was something that Labour's own plans did not try to counter.

Could Labour's plans really be that badly off target? When the votes were counted, the answer was reassuringly confirmed: yes.

A less happy experience was had when one of us discussed the poster plans with a campaign team that feared the momentum was slipping away from it. Some very simple mathematics quickly showed a problem. Take the number of posters the campaign team wanted up, divide by the number of days until polling day and then work out how many had to be put up per hour by the poster team, and you got a number even a superhero taking no toilet breaks would have struggled to meet.

The lesson in both cases was the same: very simple mathematics is a key campaign planning tool, as it helps you work out if plans are plausible or not, if objectives are achievable or not and what extra capacity you need to get into your campaign team and at what rate.

How many hours of door knocking will it take to hit your voter ID targets, for example? Throw in the number of possible canvassers and you quickly get a useful guide to how much effort is needed to recruit more canvassers or put on more canvassing sessions.

Often there will be many estimates and significant margins of error involved in these sorts of calculations. That does not undermine their usefulness, because the real value comes from knowing the order of magnitude of the figures involved. In the poster case, for example, it did not matter whether the true figure for the number of posters put up per hour was half or double or even treble the estimate, the point was that, regardless, it was way beyond what was plausible and so something had to be done. Likewise, whether it is 234 deliverers you need or 259, it matters not that much if you know you currently have 106; big expansion plans are needed either way.

So remember – use maths to check your plans are plausible and to guide you away from having implausible assumptions at the heart of your plans. Otherwise, when you do fail to meet them, your campaign will be in deep trouble.

CHAPTER 41

TAKING CARE OF YOUR DATA

*You can't stop things going wrong; you can
stop them turning into disasters.*

An office wall used to show a cartoon with two drunks slumped in an alleyway bemoaning their fate. One was saying to the other, 'It all started to go wrong when I realised the backups hadn't been working...' He at least had been trying to use backups.

Sometimes people fear trusting data to computers, worried that a wrong key press may result in valuable information being lost. That is to get things wrong: data is safer on computers because it is much easier to do regular backups. Data stored any other way is difficult to back up; reams of photocopies are no match for the simplicity of a computer backup. If you want your data to be safe, put it on a computer and then do regular, proper backups.

Remember, too, that storing backups is getting easier as data technology develops. 'Hard' storage devices such as external hard drives or simple USB sticks give you relatively cheap, mobile storage capacity with substantial memory space. The development of cloud computing is adding new possibilities. Even simple solutions like emailing data to yourself can provide an effective backup solution.

The best way of ensuring backups are done

effectively is to have a regular backup cycle, and stick to it regardless of how much or how little data has been added or altered since the last backup. Sticking to a regular cycle is far easier than the vagaries of doing backups as and when someone thinks it is time to do one. Make sure everyone's work is part of the cycle, especially if you have multiple offices and people working from home.

When doing backups make sure they are comprehensive – including all the ancillary information and not just the main files. A good example of when backups go wrong for campaigns is when people remember to backup their website regularly – but only backup the stories in the database and not the images that go with them (which are usually stored separately on the web server).

Keep backups for a long time. Just because you have done a new backup successfully does not mean the previous one is no longer useful. There may be a problem hidden away that you do not discover for days or even months. At that point, you need to have an old, good backup still knocking around.

Put backups in a different place from the original data. It is easy to overlook, but a backup stored right next to the original means fire, theft or another disaster that takes out the original data will almost certainly get the backup too. Sending backups securely over the internet or doing something as simple as putting them on a USB stick and then taking them to a different physical location deals with that. Check the backups actually work and contain data too.

Remember that valuable data covers more than just records of, say, party preferences of voters. We know of at least one unfortunate PhD student who lost three years' work when the only copy of his thesis was lost. A data management strategy should cover more than just 'stuff that is made up of numbers'.

You also need to plan effectively for managing data that is gathered and accessed by more than one person. Simple and effective methods for doing this have been around for decades: using a token system for identifying who has the master copy, for example. A whole range of software applications increasingly build in collaborative working capacity, so make sure you check that functionality as you expand the team of people who have access to your data.

Most of all have a plan that captures all aspects of data management, from entry to backup. Otherwise, you too could end up like the cartoon drunk in the alleyway bemoaning a backup that was running but not working. That is not a future to aspire to.

CHAPTER 42

RAISING MONEY

Nothing should impede the truth save a substantial sum of money. Hilaire Belloc

Money may not be able to buy you love, but it can buy you a bulk order of extra campaigning resources. Fundraising comes in two forms – straightforward donations, such as a response to an appeal letter; and the profit on events or activities, such as from selling tickets to social events or income from auctions.

In our experience, only a few people actively like fundraising, which makes for two common mistakes in a campaign: first, not doing enough fundraising and second, even when it is done, doing it apologetically or impersonally. It also means that effective fundraisers are, themselves, like gold dust and should be treasured and nurtured.

Our advice is to ask often, to challenge yourself to do the difficult thing and to be creative. One of the most successful campaigns that Ed worked on combined long hard graft by the candidate asking for individual donations with set-piece donor events and effective social events. The campaign attracted the support of two highly effective 'compères' who were used to great effect to run auctions and appeals at rallies and meetings. It also opted to run a huge annual fundraising fete that was open to the public. It required a high degree of organisation and planning from a team of volunteers but the funds it raised more than repaid that effort.

Because money is so important for funding campaign activity, it has to be seen as a priority for campaign managers, with the candidate in particular taking the lead – especially when it comes to soliciting larger donations (on which, see Chapter 43). Indeed, in the United States it is well established that fundraising consumes the bulk of the candidate's time.

Some money will come in with little effort, but certainly not enough. Almost all comes in because someone asked either directly, such as by making a fundraising phone call, or indirectly, such as by selling raffle tickets at a social event.

Not only does asking determine if people give, it determines how much people give – for very few people give more than they are asked. It can be tempting, particularly if you do not like fundraising, to pitch the request for funds low, with the result that you get a small donation. That misses out on the bigger sums people would have given if only they had been asked to give more.

Asking for the right sum varies from person to person, of course, based on their enthusiasm for the candidate and their disposable income (which can be very different from their apparent wealth – for example a large family in an expensive house may not have as much spare cash at the end of each month as you might think). Split your supporters into different groups based on how much they should be asked for and then keep records on how much people have given. In future you can prioritise those who have given before (as once you have given, you are more likely to give again) and tweak future requests to fit previous donations – add a little more, of course, to keep on pushing up towards the maximum they are happy with.

Appeals work best when you give people a reason for giving as well as a sense of what their donation would buy – which is why matching up possible donations with different items of expenditure is very popular. People also like to give to successful campaigns, so always report back regularly on fundraising and other progress.

Appeals also work best when you do not take the first 'no' as being final. Some people will not or cannot give anything. There are far more who will say 'no' first time (or just ignore the request) but when asked again, politely but persistently, do subsequently give.

Build fundraising into all elements of your communication strategy. A leaflet that goes through a door without asking for donations is a wasted opportunity. Ask often, build the donor base and you will find that the more campaigning you do the more money you raise. Do little and rarely ask for financial support and you will find yourself constantly campaigning on a shoestring.

CHAPTER 43

BIG DONORS

When raising money, don't forget to ask for the money.
Senator Lamar Alexander

For perfectly understandable reasons people worry about big donors and their involvement with politicians. Business people in particular are expected to view a donation as a commercial transaction – buying influence in return for their cash. It is healthy for this level of concern to exist but it should not prevent a candidate seeking large donations – in fact many donors contribute to campaigns without expecting influence in return. Even rich people can be altruistic. If you doubt that, just take a look around at the many philanthropic causes outside of politics supported by rich people.

A candidate can take three simple steps to avoid the ethical problems that might arise when accepting large donations. First, be transparent: obviously you will comply with the legal requirements for declaring donations but consider not simply doing the legal minimum. Secondly, be explicit. Make it clear to donors that contributions to your campaign have to be made with no strings attached. Third, stick to your word. Treat all voters equally in terms of the power of their voice.

So, on to some practical tips. As we discussed in

Chapter 42, the candidate must be central to fund-raising. There is nothing to beat a personal request from a candidate and, with limited time and plenty of other demands on it, it makes sense for a candidate to prioritise spending their time directly asking the people likely to give the largest sums.

Before the candidate approaches any such people, the campaign should carefully check out their background for any possible ethical problems or political embarrassments. That should be followed up later if and when a donation is actually made or about to be made with a direct question to the donor about any possible problems – a wise donor understands the implications for them, too, if a donation goes bad.

For big donors, it should be a face-to-face request. A good process that works for many is to invite a small group of possible donors to meet the candidate for lunch or dinner, with the follow-up being personal requests from the candidate to each of them for a one-to-one. If the candidate is relatively new to the scene, it can be an added draw to have a VIP guest along for the donors to meet.

Whether meeting donors individually or in a group, make sure the candidate (and the VIP) knows the 'pitch' – exactly what the campaign needs and why the donors should plug the gap. You can support this with simple but professional-looking material which might, for example, set out the campaign plan in a format similar to a business plan.

Make your pitch but remember to ask for the money (as Senator Alexander reminds us). Candidates often shy away from asking directly, but donors appreciate it – both because it flatters them and also because they know what is going to happen. Too much evasion and prevarication just gets them annoyed and impatient. (Mark remembers being on the receiving end of a pitch from a candidate who completely failed to ask for the money. As a result, Mark didn't give any.)

To identify the list of people to initially approach, think about friends and family of the candidate, generous donors from the past, current donors (or supporters) who are likely to have significant disposable cash and ask donors to suggest other donors. Ask your key supporters for people they would recommend for an approach. Few donations of any size will come 'out of the blue'. Even small individual donations in response to direct mail campaigns will often be the result of a relationship you have built with the donor (even if the relationship is only via letters and leaflets).

Often, the larger the donation, the more the donor will want to know in detail about how their money will be used. So be prepared. To secure repeat donations and further recommendations the investment needs to go beyond the first time they give money.

Every large donation can help you reach out to a wider audience with your message which, of course, will include a request for them to support your campaign in whatever way they can. In other words, more money means you can reach more people, thereby involving more people in politics and winning you more votes.

CHAPTER 44

LOGISTICS MANAGEMENT

It takes as much energy to wish as it does to plan.
Eleanor Roosevelt

Take a tour of Hollywood's version of election campaigns and there are basically three types of character involved: the chisel-chinned charismatic candidate who strides the stage making a difference; the back-room spinmeister who uses his (he is almost always male) cunning to sucker the press and the public into backing his candidate; the naïve and idealistic volunteer who often becomes disillusioned and sometimes marries the candidate.

It is hard to think of any Hollywood appearance for the campaign logistics manager. Logistics management is a bit like a sewer. Not many people talk about it; it is easy to overlook; but when it goes wrong, you most certainly notice the problems. Neither of us has any pretention to cinematic stardom yet both agree that they were better qualified for a job with UPS than a role in *The West Wing*.

A hard-fought election campaign can be a monster to manage. It will mean co-ordinating a large team of volunteers. It will mean liaising with large commercial entities that are not used to dealing with ramshackle temporary organisations which have few professional staff but make large demands on suppliers. It means dealing with small but highly skilled and sometimes temperamental suppliers whose goodwill is often stretched to the limit by the campaign's eccentric demands. Most of all it means staying focused on a single objective and all that goes into achieving it. It takes a set of very specific skills that are usually only noticed by others when something goes wrong.

Tips on effective logistics management crop up throughout this book when we talk about how to organise volunteers and get your message across. At its most basic, getting logistics right is all about having the right supplies in the right place at the right time. In other words, it is about planning and forethought.

Good logistics management can save your campaign money but mostly it is about spending resources (not just money) efficiently – and sometimes that means spending more. Let us take your computer printer as our parable. Computer printers need tender loving care at the best of times but especially so when they are being stretched far beyond the manufacturer's recommended print rate by the demands of a campaign. Have you got someone looking after your printer all the way through its monster print run? Does that person know how to fix basic problems and do they know what to do with the letters once they are printed? Do they know how to get hold of the engineer if they need to? Toner cartridges are expensive so it is tempting not to hold many in stock, but do you know how many letters they will print before they do run out? Most critically, can you get hold of replacements at 2 a.m. on a Sunday? Oh, and what is the plan if the campaign manager decides the page break is in the wrong place and the whole batch needs to be re-done?

Logistics management is not Hollywood but it is essential. There are four key steps to good logistics management: identify each key task before the campaign begins; choose the right person for the job of managing each key task; make sure they know the campaign plan with its demands and deadlines and how the task they are managing fits in; make sure they factor in a sensible margin for contingencies.

Political campaigns are unpredictable, fast moving and reliant on goodwill far more than most business operations. At the same time, there is no space for catch-up: your delivery date (election day) is not subject to negotiation. Effective logistics management goes a long way to ensuring you deliver on your objectives.

EACH ELECTION IS
A BUILDING BLOCK

*A journey of a thousand miles must begin with
a single step*. Chinese proverb

Both authors were closely involved in campaigns that took years to reach the point of victory. Liberal Democrat candidate Norman Lamb won election to Parliament for North Norfolk eleven years after first agreeing to stand as a favour to his mother. She was the formidable chair of the local party association, which had been looking for someone to carry the party's banner in the wake of the disastrous merger between the Liberal Party and the SDP.

Soon after Norman was selected as a candidate, a vacancy arose on the local council in a ward that had not been contested by the party in recent memory. A candidate was found and the local party decided to 'give it a go'. Other parties were campaigning hard in the area too but the Liberal Democrat won by no more than a couple of dozen votes. The result triggered a string of local council election wins for Lib Dem candidates that peppered the years between 1990 and Norman's eventual victory in the parliamentary contest of 2001.

Momentum was created and over the years, a team

was built. Candidates of different parties around the country can tell a similar story.

Other elections that take place in the same area, but before your own polling day, are a chance to help build up a wider team and organisational structure – assuming of course that there are friendly candidates standing in them. Tasks such as building up leaflet delivery networks, assembling email lists and accumulating voting intention data can very rarely be done well in just the one election. Stringing together progress from different elections brings many advantages.

Other elections are an invaluable opportunity for you to learn. You can develop your own skills and those of your campaign team but also grow your knowledge and understanding of the area, and the views and needs of voters.

Moreover, if friendly candidates win, then they gain public platforms which they can use in turn to help you – and the more help you have given them, the more help they are likely to give you in return. It may well be the case that they can do practical things to help with issues you are campaigning on. If you are campaigning to improve housing, for example, there is nothing to beat winning an election that sees an ally ending up on a local council in charge of that policy area.

Other interim campaigns also provide the opportunity to talent-spot and train: who are the good organisers, who are the good volunteers, who are the good planners and so on – and who is not one of those yet but shows potential? Campaigners and helpers learn and refine their skills over different campaigns, so the more you see your campaign as being part of a longer sequence of campaigns the better the flow of experiences and growth in knowledge.

Remember, too, that all these benefits to you also apply to those who are, or are likely to be, seeking election after you – this is a good group of people to involve given that extra appeal.

It is the rare candidate whose political aims can all be met simply by their own election (and if that is you, may we humbly suggest you crashing to defeat will best serve society?). More victories for more like-minded colleagues will help bring about the changes you seek.

CHAPTER 46

TIME IS A RESOURCE

The key is not in spending time, but in investing it.
Stephen R. Covey

From the complexities of Stephen Hawking's *Brief History of Time* through to the sweet innocence of a young child asking 'Where does time go when it is past?', there are many mysterious and philosophical things to be said about the nature of time. In political campaigns, it boils down to two brutal, inescapable facts: there is not enough time and you cannot move polling day to make more.

The immovable nature of polling day makes for a sort of deadline that is rare in many other occupations. Commercial suppliers with apparently impeccable pedigrees have struggled with polling day's immovability. Consider a major new car launch by comparison. Heads may roll and sales may be lost if the new car cannot be launched on time, but in the end you can delay the launch. Polling day is not like that.

The scarcity of campaigning time means that often time is not invested in sensible ways. When you are busy it is always tempting to cut out those things that do not deal directly with the immediate pressing demands. That means time to recruit more helpers and train up new or existing people to do their roles better is often sacrificed. It should not be.

A wise investment of time that increases the campaign's overall capacity ends up saving time. From simple training that speeds up someone's computer skills (one of the authors once timed an Excel task with a colleague; what had taken the colleague over an hour took us less than ten minutes) to more advanced training that lets a new person take on some of the work that a hard-pressed existing team member is drowning in, wise investment of time produces fantastic returns.

Effective delegation is a challenge for many people. Because a candidate or a campaign manager cannot do everything needed to win, it is essential to invest time in finding the right people to delegate to and help them to learn how to complete the tasks they are given effectively. It is also important to put in place the systems that are needed to monitor progress in key tasks.

Prioritising is another challenge for the best of us. One of the most common time errors that we have seen among election candidates is choosing to prioritise tasks that would only really be a priority once they are elected. Attendance at a particular committee might make good copy for a campaign story. The first couple of times it might be time well spent on networking with opinion formers. But, beyond that, if it is not your job to be there, is your campaign really getting any value from your attendance? (Gathering intelligence on topical issues might be useful but could you do this via a thirty-minute phone call with a member of the committee?)

We all understand the importance of saying no sometimes, but what is the best way to do it? Often, for a candidate, it can work best if you have someone else to say no on your behalf – a staffer or volunteer who runs your diary, for example, who you can refer enquiries to. It is important if you are delegating this task to make sure you give that person a clear briefing on what tasks or events you want to accept and why and which ones you will want to decline.

For the candidate there is another priority: there also needs to be a special emphasis on making sure their time is not only spent on what will help win but also on what only they, the candidate, can do. Some general mucking in with tasks such as clerical work in the office can be good for team bonding and morale. However, do not lose sight of the biggest priorities: only the candidate can walk out on stage at a debate for candidates and only a candidate can do the practice sessions ahead of that event.

PART 4

COMMUNICATING
YOUR MESSAGE

Now you have a message (Part 1), the team (Part 2) and resources (Part 3), it is time to look at how you use these to get your message across. Effective communication is at the core of any winning election campaign. Whatever your message, it is worthless if people are not hearing it.

CHAPTER 47

UNDERSTAND YOUR AUDIENCE

*A politician's words reveal less about what he thinks about
his subject than what he thinks about his audience.*
George Will

The most charismatic candidate, the most effective campaign plan, will deliver you few votes if you fail to communicate with the electorate. At the core of our approach to communicating your message is a simple note: you might dream of persuading everyone to vote for you but you will not. Fortunately, to win, you do not have to. What you do need to do is to find the most efficient and effective way of getting your message across to the people who will consider voting for you, then keep talking to them until you persuade them.

Behind that message is another: it is vitally important to understand those potential supporters. Do not assume they think like you and your campaign team. Do not assume they read the same newspapers (or, indeed, any newspapers) or share the same obsessions. Do not assume they will even agree with you on every single issue: they almost certainly will not.

Multiple networks make up most people's lives today. They interact with those networks in different ways at different times and they are influenced by them in a variety of ways. It is dangerous to make assumptions about the outlook of voters based on very broad categories. After all, pensioners in the UK, for example, will include some who first cast their vote in the 'Hungry 30s' and others who first voted at the height of 1960s 'Flower Power'. This matters because it means you cannot treat voters as a vast, unchanging, homogeneous audience. You need to invest resources into developing a real understanding of how voters think and why.

A good route to understanding your (possible) voters – what interests them and what channels of communication they prefer – is to create a few imaginary personas that typify them and who you can then think about when making decisions. Perhaps one might be 'Anna', a middle-aged woman living in the suburbs with kids at a local school who reads a Sunday newspaper and is in a part-time job. Imagining Anna and how best to communicate with and appeal to her is much easier than thinking of abstract information and data tables of demographics, media consumption and the like.

Come up with a set of personas and make sure all of those who make campaign decisions know who these people are. In particular, make sure the campaign then reaches out to where these people are – if they are heavy readers of the local newspaper, you need to put extra effort into local newspaper work; if they are heavy supporters of the local sports teams, then spending time leafleting outside their matches starts to make sense.

In doing this, remember that women make up the majority of the electorate. Read much about campaigning and the chances are you will come across references to 'winning the women's vote', 'how women voted' and so on. Treating the majority as if they are a special, different group of people is rather odd, isn't it? That is because politics have traditionally been dominated by men (just look at the gender balance of those who get elected) and so treat women, the majority, as if they are somehow the different ones (or forget to think about women voters at all).

A successful campaign will work out who the voters are that are most likely to support them whatever their characteristics and will talk to those people (in the most fine-grained way possible) about the issues that affect them. That way you will not bore them but persuade them.

CHAPTER 48

SINGLE-ISSUE CAMPAIGNING

A single-issue campaign brings multiple benefits.

Why wait until after polling day to show you can make a difference? Successful campaigns build momentum and candidates build a record well before voters go to the polls. Representing people is an effective way of building support and it is the right thing to do.

Twenty years ago, Ed helped to organise a community campaign to save a library. It deployed a range of tactics which all involved residents in the campaign: from displaying a window poster, to signing a postcard, to 'use it or lose it' sign-up campaigns, even a picket of the library when the committee making the decision came to visit. It remains a favourite campaign and the library itself remains open to this day. Importantly, it breathed new campaigning life into the local political party organisation and reinforced a strong record of community representation for the team of councillors and candidates.

As well as building a reputation for your candidate, offering many learning opportunities for campaigners and improving local representation, single-issue campaigning can help to keep your campaign team motivated. Some people do get pleasure from leaflet delivery. In our experience, though, offering nothing but that, month after month for a decade in the hope that eventually it might be possible to make a difference, is not the most effective way to motivate campaign volunteers. Well-run community campaigns can be fun – if they are inclusive and inventive and led by people who know how to motivate. If they deliver a winning result, that is even better!

As an added benefit, delivering real outcomes brings credibility and support. You can (indeed must) still do the more partisan political messages. But with a proven record of representing voters behind you, those messages are more likely to be believed and there will more likely be helpers to distribute them.

Having campaigning that is rooted in the wider community's concerns and activities is also a good insurance policy against 'turning native' when you do have power. It keeps you in touch with your voters' concerns. It protects you against heading off in whichever way the winds blow – or from being pushed there by well-meaning bureaucrats and (sometimes less well-meaning) party bosses. Getting people's participation and input gives you an independence of purpose – and means you are more likely to set the right objectives.

It also protects against slipping into 'activism without a purpose', where the only objectives and plans are around leaflets and votes rather than about changing the area for the better, and the outcome frequently is disillusion and people dropping out of political activism.

There is not much point in simply winning an election and joining the establishment – it will carry on quite OK without you, thank you. Having firm beliefs and convictions about what needs to change is another matter. So between now and polling day, make sure you run mini-campaigns on individual issues which produce improvements for the community.

Identifying issues to pick up is relatively easy in almost all communities – as long as you are in regular dialogue with the public. Individual pieces of case-work, which are symptomatic of wider problems, often provide good prompts for such issues – though you must be very careful to respect individual people's privacy and preferences. More widely, getting people to ask on the doorstep and on the phone, along with surveys delivered through letterboxes and chances for people to submit views online, should give you plenty of raw material to work with.

Single-issue campaigns that are grounded in your community will help make your own campaign grow and keep you in touch with local concerns. If you can save a library along the way, what's not to love about them?

CHAPTER 49

DELIVERY NETWORKS

What you won't learn from The West Wing.

Volunteers regularly hand-delivering pieces of literature to voters in their homes (through their letterboxes in most countries, though notably not the US with the legal restrictions around touching people's letterboxes) is a core way for campaigns to get their messages to the public.

It does not come with the expense of advertising and, unlike many advertising mediums, you can target precisely who you want to communicate with. In addition, you won't waste money on publicity that is seen by people who do not even live in the right place.

It still costs money to produce the literature that your volunteers deliver, but it cuts out what is normally the biggest financial cost – that of distribution.

Building up a good network usually takes time. Think of it as an investment in the future and start asking supporters today. Then keep on asking and gradually, over time, the delivery network fills out. Even if you are campaigning on a national scale, your campaign organisation has to be able to function on a micro scale.

It is best to split the addresses in the area into chunks that take thirty to sixty minutes to deliver. Supporters will find the time to complete this sized task. Be flexible about these delivery rounds – make the rounds suit where people live and where they would like to deliver.

When you give a volunteer their delivery round, include a note that clearly states which addressees to deliver to, when the leaflets need to be delivered by and contact details so the volunteer can report back. The report should let you know the delivery is complete and provide any extra information, e.g. if they spot a local issue that needs fixing or find a supporter. A nice tip is to put all the names who report back into a small prize draw each time – that way one deliverer gets a small 'thank you' prize and all of them get into the habit of letting you know when they have done their delivery, which can be very useful for managing the team and spotting problems.

Over time you can add in more detail on the slips, such as 'flat A at number 34 is round the back on the right' or 'odd numbers are over the shops; look out for the doors at the car park entrance'.

As the number of deliverers grows, a new role becomes useful: the wholesaler. This person will collect the bundles of leaflets from the campaign and take them to each deliverer. Expecting your deliverers to come to you to get leaflets just means fewer people will do it; get the leaflets to them.

In areas with heavy traffic congestion, good wholesalers often build up a rapport with their deliverers and agree where they can leave the leaflets for them, so they can nip round very early or very late when the streets are free of traffic. That makes the job far quicker.

Deliverers are so important they should be regularly thanked. Invite them to all the local social events (even if they are not paid-up party members), feature and thank them in member/supporter news-letters, give a regular prize draw (see above) and regularly give feedback on the impact of the literature they are delivering – especially if it includes a petition or survey whose progress can be reported.

Volunteer deliverers and efficient delivery networks rarely get any media coverage, rarely feature in TV shows and films, and are rarely mentioned in political speeches. This hugely under-estimates their impor-tance: you need them if you are going to win.

CHAPTER 50

BUILDING YOUR OWN MEDIA

You too can be a media mogul.

The 'Focus' newsletter was invented by Liberals during the party's post-war nadir because, with few elected public offices and with very little sympathy for the party among media owners and editors, the party needed its own way of distributing news about its activities. A regular newsletter – delivered all year round, election time or not – was the answer.

Regular newsletters – for any party – can still deliver those benefits of having your own mini-media empire in an area. Indeed, technological change has increased their potential in many areas because it has weakened the circulation and resources of many local and regional newspapers. This means that in many places local newsletters can find a welcome audience because there is so little good local news available from the traditional media.

Technological change has also opened up new possibilities for candidates and political parties to build up their own media network in an area. Whether it is a popular email newsletter – as former Labour MP Nick Palmer ran very successfully in Broxtowe – or a well-read blog – as current Liberal Democrat MP Lynne Featherstone has shown – it is possible to become one of the main sources for local news in an area.

Of course, the objective of a candidate is not to become a media mogul but to win elections and implement policies, so retain a healthy mix between news about your own activities and other news of interest to people in the area. The best news sources combine the two, for example, providing information on changes to public transport timetables because of engineering work or changed contracts, alongside news about campaigning to improve public transport.

Too much about you and your interests, and people will not find you an interesting source of news, so you will not build up an audience. Too little about what you are doing and you end up providing a community service, but not helping to win elections. Success comes from getting the balance right.

This same principle applies regardless of the medium – whether it is paper, email, Facebook, blogs or something else. Which medium is most appropriate depends on what the competition is out there. Some areas have very well-established and successful community news blogs, others have popular discussion forums, yet others have very well-read local newspapers. The trick is to look at the media landscape – online and offline, traditional and new – and to spot the appropriate gap(s) your own efforts can look to fill.

Then it is a matter of building up the audience – which is often a steady, long-term process so an early start is advisable. The reward, however, is very significant: being able to communicate with the public as and when you want to, without the editorial filtering of an intermediary. For an increasing number of MPs, the size of their direct online audience now exceeds the readership of the local newspapers in their area: that is a significant shift and one you should look to benefit from, too.

Traditional media are still important, but there is no reason to leave the field just to them. Stake your claim to part of it, too.

CHAPTER 51

LEAFLETS WITH IMPACT

How to pass the three-seconds test.

Plenty of kitchen table campaigners get a kick out of producing their own campaign literature. For all of us, though, sometimes it does not quite work out the way we wanted. To get their message across, leaflets must achieve the maximum impact in the shortest possible time. Hours may be spent on lovingly crafting a leaflet, but when it goes through someone's door, even if it escapes being scrunched to destruction by a badly designed letterbox or chewed apart by a pet dog, it usually has a very short life span. Typically, a leaflet has just three seconds to grab someone's interest as they lift it up from the doormat or out of the letterbox – three seconds in which the decision is made to read it further or to place it in the bin.

That is why simple, large and interesting headlines are so important – they are the first (and possibly only) thing looked at. Writing good short headlines is a skilled art and is one reason why other journalists hold the very best of tabloid headline writers in high esteem for their technical skills.

There are, however, a few basic pieces of advice that can stand even the beginner headline writer in good stead.

First, understand that it is a skill to be learned and

improved – headline writing should not be a hurried after-thought.

Second, make the headline answer the question for the reader 'Why should I be interested in this?' Shock-horror headlines are not the only way to achieve this. More banal headlines do the job well if the topic really is of interest to your voters, e.g. 'Village train station closing for six months.'

Third, avoid jargon, acronyms and statistics unless the meaning is extremely clear. The occasional acronym is meaningful – 'NATO' is a good example where using the acronym is actually clearer than using the full version. But do not fool yourself into thinking that just because people immersed in politics are used to a word or acronym the public is, too.

Fourth, keep headlines as short as possible. Once you have written a headline, leave it for a little while, then come back and try to edit it with the simple objective of making it one word shorter. You will be amazed how often it is possible to remove a word on the second attempt even if you were sure the headline was ultra-concise first time round.

Beyond the headlines, research shows the next most common things for readers to look at are the photographs and their captions. That makes the wording of photograph captions the second most important pieces of writing for a leaflet, after the headlines. So, again, treat them with the care and attention they deserve. The choice of photograph is important too (see Chapters 20 and 58), but a good rule of thumb is never to use a photo without an accompanying caption.

A good test of a leaflet is to give it to someone for a few seconds, take it away and ask them what they can remember of it. If it is not the main message you want to get over, re-write it, don't print it.

Finally, remember that your headline needs to work harder than a tabloid sub-editor's. Newspaper readers have bought the paper so have a degree of commitment to reading it. You need to get the core of your message across as quickly as possible. While it might be tempting to use huge one-word headlines, do they really tell people the whole of your story? Using sub-headings can help to complete the story: 'Village station to close – Jo Candidate leads protest.'

Above all, remember that no one owes you the time to read your message. Invest in getting it right so that you make it as easy for voters to 'get it' as possible. They will repay you in the ballot box.

CHAPTER 52

DIRECT MAIL MUST BE READ

*The art of writing a good letter is the
art of telling a good story.*

Direct mail is a powerful campaign tool because it lets you deliver a tailored message direct to an individual voter.

Personally addressed items get higher readership than unaddressed leaflets and are also more effective where many people share the same letterbox. The different printing technologies and means of delivering involved also mean that it is much easier to vary the content of a letter from person to person than it is to vary a leaflet from letterbox to letterbox.

Smart use of data to target the right messages to the right people can lead to very sophisticated direct mail plans, but at heart the secret of successful direct mail is very simple: it is all about the power of the story the letter has to tell.

The best letters have one point to make, and only one. The point might be made very briefly – even in just a sentence or two – or at length – letters stretching over several sides of paper can be very effective. The story must be relevant to the reader and make clear why the voter should care about your position on the issue.

Letters, like leaflets, have to fight for attention

among a public generally not that interested in political missives, so the opening should be attention grabbing. A very popular approach is to have something the reader will agree with in the first sentence. Then continue with short words, short sentences and short paragraphs.

Writing an eye-catching opening paragraph is vitally important. If you are stuck, do not let it put you off: write about the first thing you think of then move on to the second paragraph – it is a great way to overcome writer's block. You can revise the opening once the rest of the letter is written. Even if you are happy with the opening, take a second look at it. Once you have written the letter, read through it to see if you have a better opening paragraph further down. If you have to, do not be afraid to move it up to the top.

If the letter is more than one side long, have the page break appear mid-sentence at an interesting point, so people turn over to keep reading. Make sure the final sentence summarises the letter's message – as people often skip to the end of the letter before deciding whether to read it in full. Include a call to action – never miss the chance to get someone new involved in your campaign.

Give careful thought to a 'PS' – research shows it is a highly read part of a letter. It should summarise the core of your message in a single sentence.

Avoid fake handwriting fonts like the plague – they look dreadful and are horribly counter-productive. Use genuine handwriting for the signature.

Use bold, underlining and sub-headlines with caution. Sparing use of them really makes parts of the letter stand out. Too much becomes deadening to the eyes and ends up not highlighting anything.

Make sure someone pays careful attention to the production qualities of the letter and checks sample letters at every stage of the production. Sending letters to dead people because you used the wrong data or addressing women as men or having addresses that don't show through the window of a window envelope are all the sorts of mistakes that slip in if you do not take proper care over details.

Direct mail usually works best if it includes some way that people can respond, such as by giving a donation, signing a petition or completing a mini-survey. This response mechanism may be at the end of the letter or in a separate reply slip included in the envelope. Either way, make sure the reply instructions are clear and preferably include a postage-free return address.

Remember the importance of building a relationship with voters. If someone responds to a direct-mailshot campaign, follow it up with regular updates on the progress of the campaign you are running.

Finally, test your direct mail (see Chapter 11), for even very small details can make a big impact on the effectiveness of letters. Testing helps you make your letters the best they can be.

CHAPTER 53

SURVEYS THAT
ARE RETURNED

*An unreturned survey is like an unread book – it can
give the author a sense of satisfaction but the rest
of the world carries on as if it had not existed.*

There is much cynicism about 'focus group politics' but the facts are as plain as the nose on your face: if you do not listen to your voters, you will lose. The best way of finding out what your voters are saying is to ask them. Speaking to voters helps achieve this, but has the downside of being relatively slow and often, especially on the doorsteps, people are keen to keep conversations short. Opinion polling, when done well, can also help, but is expensive to do properly – and lethally misleading when done badly.

Both leaflets (Chapter 51) and direct mail (Chapter 52) should include 'response mechanisms', that is elements the public can return, such as petition forms or donation slips or other calls to action that encourage people to get in touch via a website or email. However, to get under the skin of what people are thinking in an area, to gather prominent issues and casework to help with – and to collect all-important data – there is no substitute for the dedicated survey.

The highest response rates to surveys come from 'knock and drop' surveys, where volunteers go door knocking and hand a survey form over to people they find in or deliver it through the letterbox if no one is at home. Where someone is in, they are asked to fill it out there and then, and then leave it half-sticking out of the letterbox, so the volunteer can call past again in thirty minutes or so and pick it up without having to disturb them again. The survey also has a freepost return address in case people cannot fill it in straightaway or they are out when the volunteer calls.

This method of surveying is very effective, but is time-consuming. An alternative is to deliver surveys like direct mail – with mail-merged name and address on, and which people can post back. A good trick is to leave the envelope unsealed so that people can fold the survey back into the envelope and use that to post it back. You will be surprised what a big obstacle finding an envelope can be for some people! You can even artwork the survey so that people can re-fold the leaflet and have the return address showing through the window envelope, so they do not even have to address it.

The final version of surveying is the easiest but produces the lowest returns – no pre-printed names and addresses, no door knocking but just an unaddressed survey printed like a normal leaflet and delivered through people's doors. Surveys done this way are cheap to produce and easy to deliver in large numbers but the response rate will be very low and many will be returned anonymously.

Whatever form of survey you do, it is important to ensure that it meets the legal data protection requirements. These are not onerous, usually involving a simple piece of regulatory text on the survey with the requirement to take good care of the surveys and respondents' data and not to use it for non-political purposes. Political parties usually have their data protection registration already sorted for you and can advise on the details.

Ensure the questions not only ask for the information you will find useful and can follow up on (e.g. if any roads need repairs) but phrase them in such a way that the public can understand the reason for asking them. This will help with response rates. To understand the responses people give to questions about education or transport, it is useful to know if people have children. People will be far more willing to answer that question if it is right next to a question about schools rather than on its own somewhere else in the survey.

Finally, just as with direct mail in the previous chapter, remember that if someone returns your survey they are starting a relationship with you that you need to continue. Keep them updated on the action you have taken on the issues they have said they care about. Don't forget to ask them to help with your campaigning efforts too.

CHAPTER 54

HOW MUCH IS TOO MUCH?

Why you must learn to hate trees.

Leaflets work. Many leaflets work better. One winning campaign we worked on saw 200,000 leaflets delivered by the volunteer team to the 50,000 households on election day alone.

It is not always a popular approach with campaigners. Indeed, chances are at some point you will hear a member of the public complain, 'I'm fed up with all these election leaflets.' So why do some campaigners talk about delivering so many leaflets and letters to voters?

Imagine you are on the doorstep trying to persuade someone to vote for you. Even if the conversation goes really well, it is hard to persuade anyone of anything in less than ninety seconds. Now, remember the three-second test (Chapter 51). If a leaflet typically gets three seconds of attention, then thirty leaflets (a large number!) only adds up to the same amount of time as that one hurried ninety-second conversation on the doorstep.

Though there is a little of apples and oranges in this comparison, it makes the point: you need a lot of pieces of paper, phone calls, emails, text messages and more to add up to much of a correspondence with the voter.

Think of another practical example: a family home containing two adults and their two teenage children. In the final week of the campaign, you are planning to deliver a leaflet at the weekend, one on Monday, one on Wednesday evening and one on Thursday morning (election day). Dad is digging the garden when you deliver the leaflet on Sunday. He picks it up from the doormat, reads it and sticks it in the recycling bin. Daughter arrives home from school before anyone else on Monday and bins your second leaflet without reading it, because she is not interested in politics. On Wednesday evening, the son is heading out to football practice as you are delivering your third leaflet. He takes it from you, glances at it and leaves it on the floor of the car where it is tidied away the following weekend. On Thursday, mum is first out of the house, picks up your final leaflet, votes on the way to work and opens your final enveloped mailing on her coffee break at work.

It is not a far-fetched scenario, is it? Four leaflets, two read, each by one person in the household, one is read three hours *after* the person has voted. And in your campaign you plan that all four people will have read four leaflets each in the last few days of the campaign.

The toleration level varies among people, which means that if nobody is complaining then you are doing less than the least tolerant person wants – and far less than the average person wants. It is only when you get a complaint or two that you are heading towards what the typical voter is happy with.

So, the really scary thing is not to hear voters complaining about too much literature; it is to hear no complaints at all.

Moreover, even if complaints are about the quantity of leaflets, what usually causes them is the quality, not the quantity. Poor quality letters and leaflets bore people much more quickly and prompt complaints about 'too much'. When the leaflets and letters are well written and lively on relevant issues, the complaints dissipate.

In other words, chop down those trees, turn them into leaflets and letters and get them through people's letterboxes as if paper were going out of fashion.

CHAPTER 55

DOOR KNOCKING

We knocked on 160,000 doors.
Labour councillor Darren Rodwell on winning
back votes in Barking from the BNP

In 2006, the far-right British National Party caused a political earthquake in Britain by winning twelve seats on Barking Council, making them the second largest party in the borough. The Labour Party locally was spurred into action and four years later Labour won every single seat on the council. Part of their success was recognising one cause of their initial failure – that they had lost touch with local voters by neglecting face-to-face contact.

So far, one golden rule has held for both the authors. Whenever we have taken someone door knocking for the first time, someone who has been worried about either meeting rude people or meeting people who want to talk about policy details they may not know, the reaction from the public has always been better than they feared. Because, in truth, nearly everyone is polite on the doorstep (and those that are not shut the door so quickly on you there is little time for them to be rude) and very few people want to talk policy at length.

Despite the public's preference for brevity on the doorstep, the public also likes having politicians call on it – or perhaps more accurately, dislikes no one calling on it. Finding someone in, especially today where more people live alone and more people are barricaded behind shared doorways, intercoms and private gated residences, is much harder than it used to be.

When calling on people there are three different sorts of calls to make. One, and the most common, is simple 'voter ID' – find out which party the people in the household are voting for (get individual answers – many households do not vote all as one) and then move on as quickly as possible to the next doorstep.

The second is the longer chat, which works particularly well for candidates, where you also deliberately spend some time talking about the issues and policy questions. After all, given it is harder to find someone in these days – and your leaflets have to compete increasingly with pizza flyers and the like – why not make the best of actually finding a human opening a door?

The third is leading with a petition or a survey – i.e. something other than simply asking voting intention. This is often a better way of starting up a conversation (and is a good way of gathering in a wider set of information than simply voting intention).

If there are two of you, make sure both have a complete set of the names and addresses to call on – so you can 'leap frog' down the same side of the street. This means each person is always near someone else, particularly important to reassure canvassers about their personal safety in less salubrious areas on dark winter nights. (Actually, neither of the authors has ever encountered a problem with personal safety when out canvassing, but reassuring people in this way is a good way of getting more people to volunteer.) If there is a large number of people, have one person with the names and addresses, giving each person in the team a door in turn to call on, and collecting their data in between sending them on to the next door. If the candidate is out with a team, then hold the candidate back to join a canvasser on the doorstep when they find someone in and willing to talk.

Door knocking is most fun when done by two or more people working the same road – so you always have a friendly face to nod at and exchange a quick word with in between doorsteps. A good tip is to encourage people to bring a friend along with them when canvassing. If they are new, they can go together door to door and, as they gain experience, you gain two helpers for the price of one. Each one knows there is a friendly face nearby, making canvassing more fun and welcoming.

However you organise the door knocking, as you go from door to door, even on the steepest slope in the worst of weather, remember one thing – 'politicians never come round here' is one of the most common complaints people make. Each door you knock on builds the reputation of democracy.

CHAPTER 56

USING THE TELEPHONE

The telephone is a good way to talk to people without having to offer them a drink. Fran Lebowitz

The telephone is an established tool in political campaigning although its use does meet resistance from some who feel uncomfortable making unsolicited calls. It is, though, too important to ignore and so you should invest time in finding a team of people who are happy to make use of the phone to help your campaign.

Compared with door knocking, telephoning has one main drawback and one main advantage. The drawback is simple – not everyone has a phone number you can get hold of (or permission to use). The advantage is that dialling the next phone number takes no longer if the person is next door to your previous call or fifty miles away. So, whether your patch is rural and the voters are dispersed, suburban with lots of long driveways, or urban where contact rates are low because people are rarely at home, the phone is a powerful tool. It is also very well suited to targeted rather than blanket contacts.

There are two different ways of organising mass phoning. One is to give out lists of names and numbers to people who make the calls in their own time, from home. This has the advantage that the callers can schedule their effort to fit their own circumstances, such as around child care duties. The drawback is that working away on your own at home misses the sociable and fun aspects of working with others. And, truth be told, sometimes good intentions can be overtaken by a host of other domestic chores.

Alternatively, you can arrange for people to meet up to do their phoning together. In the past, this used to require having a location with multiple phone lines – not always a convenient or affordable option. With increasing numbers of people having mobile phone with free minutes allowances, getting people together in this way has become much easier. Campaigns can also acquire cheap, bottom of the range 'pay-as-you-go' phones for modest sums of money. This is a good way of making sure that less well-off supporters can still help a campaign.

It is a bit like the merits of working at home versus in an office. There is no one right answer suitable for all people and all circumstances. Instead, make sure people have both options available so the right one is always available for any particular person.

There are one or two simple tips to follow when managing a telephone team. First, introduce a competitive element to spur people on. Group people into teams and give them targets for the number of contacts or key bits of data collected (such as email addresses). Find a donor who will give a meaningful prize to the winning team each month (maybe get people to buy themselves out of telephone canvassing by making the donation). Do not call too late at night (but do concentrate calls in the evening to maximise the hit rate). If possible, match the callers to their calls – if you have a Polish speaker on your team give them voters with Polish surnames, for example, or give older voters to older callers. Always have someone on hand who can deal with awkward calls with some authority – difficult questions about policy or complaints about the call itself do sometimes arise.

Make sure callers are given the tools to do a good job. Provide training so that callers make a good and interesting initial impression. Everyone should be given a script to guide what they say. It should start with them introducing themselves by name and explaining why they are calling. Put a glass of water next to the script. Remind callers to smile: if you smile when you talk, you sound friendlier even if the person is unable to see the smile.

Importantly, the candidate must remember how valuable the phone canvass is. Join the team and make sure you say thank you. Remember a winter evening spent making calls beats the cold and rainy outdoors. And on the phone, all an angry dog can do is bark at you.

CHAPTER 57

GETTING TO KNOW
JOURNALISTS

Journalists are busy human beings.

The media is another way of getting your message out and it is going through a period of immense change. Newspaper circulations are falling and new business models are being adopted. News is becoming increasingly localised thanks to the internet and the growth of 'citizen journalism'. At the same time, technology is increasing the speed of global communication. And digital communication is blurring the traditional lines between media with podcasts, vodcasts and live streaming.

All of this means that the traditional 'beat' journalist is becoming rarer and more stretched. Yet they are still an important link in your campaigning efforts.

There are three important steps to building a productive relationship with journalists. You need to get to know the journalists themselves, the news values they work to and the deadlines they face.

Most journalists are over-worked, which means they are receptive to people who help provide them with reliable information that fits with their own editorial needs – in terms of subject, timing and editorial line.

Some love statistical reports out of which a headline-grabbing number can be pulled; others hate having to look at numbers. Some might be interested in the personal stories that can liven up an issue; others look down their noses at such information.

Get to know journalists as individual people doing their jobs rather than abstract names. Do not treat them all as if they fit the cliché stereotype of the last set of journalists you saw in a TV drama or film.

One candidate we know invested time in regularly taking the political reporter covering her patch out for coffee, just to build the relationship. Another held occasional briefing sessions for a small group of journalists hosted by a visiting political personality. Either approach gives you a chance to get to know the journalist and to ask what they need from you.

Beware of treating anything as off the record, by the way. If the information is too juicy, it has a remarkable way of finding its way out, off the record or not and, anyway, journalists often have different views of what 'off the record' means – does it mean the information is not for using or just not for using with your name alongside it? American journalists often have detailed layers of classification, with information off the record, for background and more. The UK does not have similar standard formulations.

The working day and week of a journalist usually varies from relatively quiet relaxed times to an increasingly hectic workload as news deadlines approach. In those quiet periods, they are often happy to meet for an informal chat.

Processes – and deadlines – are hugely important to newspapers. Journalists are used to working fast to meet a deadline but they will not be able to help if your story comes to them after the deadline has passed! So find out what deadlines the relevant newspapers work to and plan your media events around those deadlines. Remember to ask if online editions work to different deadlines (and remember to ask, also, if they will take multimedia, e.g. video clips, for their online edition).

The biggest challenge for any candidate is making your campaign newsworthy. What we mean by that is making sure what you send to the newspaper actually matches with what they are looking for in a story.

A regular moan from politicians is that they cannot get their stories published by the newspaper. Often they blame this on editorial bias but more often than not it is because the politician has failed to understand what the newspaper needs from a story. There are some universal rules – such as topicality and the importance of a human angle to a story – but different newspapers will look for different things. The simplest way to find out what will score a hit with a journalist is to ask!

CHAPTER 58

PHOTO OPS

Remember the law of the left nostril.

We talked in Chapter 20 about the importance of powerful images to capture the campaign message. Campaigns end up consuming far more photographs than those iconic images as they are the everyday bread and butter of press work, literature and online campaigning. Facebook, for example, prioritises images when deciding what content to show in the main newsfeed panel, and photographs are one of the most looked-at parts of printed publications.

Generating plenty of good photographs is a must. Increasingly the media, especially local media, will happily use photographs that the campaign takes and supplies electronically (either via email or via photo sharing websites). If the photographer is your own, the need to be clear about what makes for a good photo is all the more important.

The most important point to remember is the law of the left nostril. Looking through photographs taken of candidates and supporters, neither Ed nor Mark has ever seen one that has triggered the reaction 'My goodness. That was taken far too close. I can see up the person's left nostril.' Numerous photographs have, however, triggered the reaction 'Who is that blob in the distance?'

However close a photographer is, they can always take an extra step forward. Always.

Photos for campaign use are very different from holiday snaps as the main purpose is reversed. In a typical holiday snap the location is more important than the people present. In a campaign photo, the people – candidate and possibly supporters – are the story, with most viewers of the photo possibly not familiar with who they are. The background is just that – the background. So get in close. Candidates photographed against big backgrounds – parliament buildings for example – are often a problem. A simple trick is to position your people some distance from the building so you can photo them close up but still capture the building, too.

Remember, too, that the photograph should send the right message. Aside from being taken from too far away, the most common mistake is to have the candidate on their own looking slightly gormlessly at the camera. There are two things wrong with this. First, a candidate on their own sends the wrong subliminal message. You want the candidate to appear popular and someone who spends time talking to people, which means a photo with more people in it. Second, staring at a camera means missing the opportunity for an action photo, with all the right and positive messages that this sort of photo sends.

As well as 'empty-field' syndrome remember the other messages that your props can send. Think of that classic image of Ronald Reagan in the 1984 presidential campaign mentioned earlier. He exposed a hole in his shoe, sending an effective message about how hard he was campaigning. We will let you decide whether it was accidental or deliberate...

To recognise the candidate easily they should be face on to the camera. But they should be active and that means looking at what they are doing. Finding the balance is key.

Follow these simple tips – and learn by critically viewing the thousands of images that appear each week in the print and online media – and you will be able to turn the missed opportunities of a distant, lonely, static figure into the sort of dynamic image that wins votes.

CHAPTER 59

PRESS RELEASES

*Like the first reports of Mark Twain's death, reports of
the end of the press release have been greatly exaggerated.*

There are many articles prophesying the immi-
nent death of the press release and they often
sound very convincing until you look at their dates.
The death of the press release has been a regular
prediction for a decade and more, yet, if you ask a
journalist, they certainly feel no shortage of press
releases coming into their email inbox. Far from it;
journalists complain about too many press releases.

Save for a name change – to news release – the press
release still has plenty of life in it as a basic communication tool with journalists.

A good press release gets information over to a journalist quickly, clearly and factually. Press releases need
to interest, but not with verbal trickery or marketing
gimmicks.

The headline should be short, clear and informative.
The sort of intriguing headlines you see on hoardings
outside newsagents that half tell you a story, but really
require you to go in and buy a paper to know what it
is about, have no place in a news release. Its headline
should be a simple factual summary of the story. The
journalist – or more likely a sub-editor – will sort out
any fancy headline; that is their job, not yours.

The first paragraph should capture the 'Five Ws'. It should tell the 'who', 'what', 'why', 'where' and 'when' of the story. In other words, give all the key information up front. This is not a nineteenth-century novel with a carefully constructed plot leading to a denouement.

The subsequent paragraphs can expand on this information, before the release ends with contact information – preferably both email and mobile phone number.

At the end, 'notes to editors' can include extra background information, such as the full details of statistics mentioned in the release.

Include in the release a quote that the journalist can use in writing up the story. It can be very hard to judge what length of quote they will use, so go for one that is several sentences long but which edits down very easily to something shorter.

Press releases these days are usually sent by email and increasingly read by journalists on their mobile phones, which means the use of fancy layouts and graphics should be kept to a minimum. You want the email to open quickly and readably before impatience and too many other emails take over, and your email is zapped before being read.

Where there are photographs to go with the story, a good idea is to put them up on a photo-sharing website such as Flickr, including a direct link to them in the release.

Think about your strategy for the press release, especially if it carries an important message. Is the story going to evolve over time – in which case are you getting the timing of the release right (should some parts of it be held back for a second bite later)? Is it something that would be better suited to a particular type of media, local TV, radio or newspaper? Can you offer a journalist an exclusive? Build in the capacity to make personal contact, too – speak to a journalist before you send the release and check with them afterwards to see if they are going to use it and if you can provide a supplementary quote.

Two concluding tips: get your facts right before you send the release and make sure anyone quoted or referred to in the release is happy to be featured (the human angle to a story is important but the humans have to be willing!).

Once again, a set of simple steps to follow and a small investment of time getting it right can hugely increase the return you get from your campaigning efforts.

CHAPTER 60

HANDLING INTERVIEWS

Death will be a great relief. No more interviews.
Katharine Hepburn

In the run-up to his eventually successful 1992 US presidential bid, Bill Clinton had worked hard to present himself as a different sort of Democrat – modern and centrist. Facing a meeting of state Democrat Party chairs in 1991, his campaign smartly planted a question to him with an audience member – not a nice question, but a tough one. Was he really 'a Republican in Democrat's clothing'? The reason? The question let him target the key issue head on. It is a classic case of good preparation – being put on the spot is something to welcome, not to shun, as long as you have a good message.

That applies just as much to media interviews. Do your prep. Work out what your main message is and what you want to achieve.

It is normal and reasonable to ask for some information in advance – who will be doing the interview, what the topic will be and what sort of story the interview is going to fit in. Find out what the format of the interview will be – will you be part of a panel or on your own; is it a pre-record or live?

Second, remember that, on most occasions, the interviewer will not be rooting for you to mess up.

The interviewer wants to get a good story out of the interview but the interview itself will not (usually) be the story. The interviewer will not want a boring interviewee with little to say so they will usually help you out as much as they can.

Third, work out your key messages in advance. Try to ensure that you get those messages across in the interview but try to avoid using a sledgehammer to force pre-prepared sound bites into an interview regardless of the questions. Many of the most notoriously awful interviews given by politicians come from politicians not only sticking to a message, but also using the same words over and over again, as if they are a stuck record, unable to think and not willing to listen. In the UK, prominent figures of both the main political parties have come unstuck in this way, most famously Michael Howard in his confrontation with Jeremy Paxman over prisons policy and Ed Miliband in his public sector strikes interview.

Fourth, make sure you are comfortable. Always arrive in good time for an interview and make sure you know where you are going. Have some water to drink (opinions differ over whether an interview goes better on a full or an empty bladder – we will let you decide that one!).

If the interview is for the radio, ask where the microphone is and make sure that you know how close or far away from it you need to be. It is acceptable to have some brief written notes with you that you might glance at now and again. Pausing for a detailed read through is not!

If the interview is for the TV, make sure you know whether to look at the interviewer or at the camera. It is usually the interviewer, unless it is a 'down the line' interview with the interviewer in a different location. TV is particularly harsh on people whose eyes move around as they talk, often making them look untrustworthy. Looking steadily at the interviewer is the answer and a good tip is to look just above the eyes, where the eyebrows meet. That makes for a less intense experience than staring directly into someone's eyes, but gives a target for the eyes that avoids the roving shifty look.

Unfortunately, giving the right impression in an interview comes not from what you say but from how you look. Neat, smart clothes and a calm, relaxed way of speaking are necessary for a good outcome.

Whether TV or radio, treat the microphones as always being live and recording. Far too many politicians have been caught out by thinking something was turned off. The answer is simple – always assume a microphone is on.

Watch out for the 'just one other thing' question. Even where journalists stick closely to the topic mentioned in advance, if there is a very timely or controversial story in the air they are likely to slip in a question about that at the end.

Finally, remember that most politicians will do at least one bad interview in their career but that the vast majority of interviews will go really well.

As with so much else in life, practice will help you master the art. Ask any seasoned interviewee and they will tell you that the secret to their success is nothing more complicated than relaxing into the role having done so many interviews.

CHAPTER 61

MAKING SPEECHES

*Never speak on a subject about which the audience
knows more than you do.* Margaret Thatcher

Great platform speeches seem to be relic of a lost
age. It is hard to imagine that many readers
of this book will make their name by matching the
soaring oratory of Martin Luther King or Winston
Churchill. Though we hope there are a few.

Of course the mechanics of political communication have changed. When Churchill was a young
journalist and cavalry officer serving with the British
army he regularly asked Conservative Party organisers
to arrange public meetings for him to address when he
was home on leave. Large crowds would come to listen
to him address town hall (or open-air) meetings as he
developed skills that he likened to those of a music
hall performer. It is difficult to imagine a large crowd
turning out today to listen to a twenty-something
adventurer hold forth on the issues of the day. More
likely, you will find yourself talking to a few friends
and colleagues about your trip overseas over a beer and
that hones conversational, not speech-making, skills.

But public speaking is still an important craft for a
politician to learn.

Phil Collins, speech writer for Tony Blair, says there
are three (of course) essential ingredients to a great

speech: a serious argument which leaves the audience thinking something new or resolved to act; great delivery that stirs the emotions as well as appealing to reason; and a sense of occasion.

The best speech makers can deliver a speech in a way that looks spontaneous, but most times the best speeches stand on a solid base of preparation. Know how long you have to speak, and work out how long that means your speech needs to be. You probably speak at around 120 to 140 words per minute so you can plan how many words you have to play with. It is hard to speak for less than five minutes. It is hard, too, to speak for much more than twenty-five minutes. Even if you do not deliver the speech from a script, it is well worth writing it out so that you can see how to structure what you have to say and ensure you get your key messages across.

Practise the delivery. Preferably with an audience (even if it is only one person).

Make sure you know the layout of the event. Where will you be speaking from and with what equipment? Will there be a panel of speakers and, if so, what are the other speakers going to say? Know who to thank and know something about them (the event organiser, the person introducing you, the other speakers).

Know the audience. Margaret Thatcher's advice at the beginning of the chapter is worth pondering – one of your authors embarrassingly delivered a speech about the European Union where he consistently referred to the wrong figure for the EU's population only to be corrected publicly at the end by one of the audience.

Will there be a question and answer session? If so, make sure you know what you are going to say to the most obvious, topical or difficult questions.

Do not say anything that you would not later be happy to see appear on YouTube (ever).

Think about props. We know of one speaker who was talking about defence issues who started his speech by taking a live bullet from his pocket and placing it on the podium. It certainly got people's attention but we do not necessarily recommend it!

There are many examples of great speeches that you can watch to spot what works best. Watch Ronald Reagan, for example, who draws on his actor training to deliver some memorable lines. One of our favourites is Mario Cuomo's response to Reagan's Shining City on a Hill speech – delivered at the 1984 Democratic Convention. Cuomo's understated delivery is full of a passion that catches the mood of the audience and clearly moves many of them to tears. A great rallying cry that can be admired for its art regardless of your politics.

Our final tip? Look on the internet for a hidden gem. Back in the 1980s the journalist Max Atkinson took a political novice and showed her all the tricks of speech making before unleashing her on a party conference to make her first ever speech. It is still highly relevant: http://maxatkinson.blogspot.com/2010/02/claptrap-movie-revisited.html

CHAPTER 62

LETTERS PAGES AND PHONE-INS

Audience participation means you.

Candidates often work incredibly hard to get media coverage yet ignore one gaping opportunity: audience participation.

It is more obvious in the form of local newspapers, where the letters page is usually one of the most well-read parts of the newspaper and only rarely is its editor flooded with good letters to choose from. Getting coverage in the news stories is certainly worthwhile, but the letters page is an open invitation.

In order to maximise the chances of getting letters published, take some time to read the letters pages over several editions. Different papers have very different styles. What sort of length of letter does the paper usually publish? Does the paper like publishing letters that are direct responses to its stories or responses to previously published letters? And, if so, does it publish responses to responses?

The importance of knowing all this is illustrated by the 2009 collection of unpublished letters to the *Daily Telegraph*, assembled for the book *Am I Alone in Thinking...?* Many of them are of a style that would be very at home in the letters pages of *The Guardian* but did not hit the different expectations of the *Daily Telegraph*.

Watch out for how promptly responses have to appear. Often if a paper happily runs responses to stories and other letters, it only does so in the edition immediately after. Check the deadlines for submitting letters and what information must be submitted alongside the letter, such as whether a full postal address is required.

Once you know all this, you can work out how quickly a letters page needs to be read (the morning the newspaper comes out or by the end of the following day?) and build that into a regular schedule for someone.

When it comes to writing letters, the usual rules of clear writing apply – short words, short sentences and short paragraphs.

A combination of research and brevity similarly applies to local radio phone-in shows. The research can take a little longer, as listening to radio shows is more time-consuming than flicking through newspaper letters pages. It is worth finding out the audience figures for the different radio shows. A mix of the officially published audience figures and asking for the data provided to would-be advertisers quickly identifies which are the most popular shows and with what sorts of audiences.

One candidate did not limit himself to political phone-ins. He cut his teeth by calling Saturday evening football phone-ins. If you know and care about football, you can no doubt talk with genuine passion about your team – just as you would want to talk with genuine passion about your political team. By trying out different approaches you can begin to work out what sort of messages and what sort of delivery works best. Remember you are broadcasting whatever the context. Do not think that because you are not talking about politics you can forget the basic rules – don't be offensive, don't swear, don't say something that you would regret if it was quoted back at you later.

Finally, don't forget the online world. Popular blogs, discussion forums and Facebook pages covering the right geographic area can be a great way of meeting the right people – but bear in mind that the need to take part in a way that fits the style and tone expected is all the more important online.

Keep looking around for opportunities to participate and your message will carry much further.

CHAPTER 63

FOLLOW THE
MEDIA COVERAGE

*Read what your voters read, watch
what your voters watch.*

It is an odd quirk that often those most involved in a campaign become only cursory readers of newspapers and rare viewers of TV. They are too busy; they have little need to read reports on something they are actively involved in; they follow the old advice that politicians should avoid obsessing over every detail of the day-by-day media coverage or stop following the media all together.

Someone, somewhere in the team, however, should be following the media in full so that you are up to speed on what the other campaigns are saying, what issues are at the top of people's minds and what new quotes or facts you can use in the campaign. It is important, too, to produce and circulate to the team relevant round-ups of media content.

A comprehensive following of the media gives a rounded picture of what is of interest to voters, without getting lost in the myopic vision of politicians only being interested in politicians. It provides a sense of the wider world, in which politics needs to make itself relevant. It can also show you what issues are bubbling up, e.g. moans about rising food prices or problems on a vital train route.

The practicalities of monitoring the media can present a logistical problem. Media of all types are becoming more decentralised. The district where Ed first campaigned falls across the circulation area of three evening local newspapers and six weekly papers, and parts will even read one of the UK's few remaining regional morning dailies. And that is just the local print media! A team of well-briefed volunteers can be a real help here: the job is not particularly demanding physically and offers the chance to combine supporting the campaign with catching up on the gossip!

Developments in digital communication can help in this part of the campaign, too. Free online news alerts are available which you can set to capture stories about your area. Even the smallest newspapers these days have online versions that you can sign up to either through an RSS feed or by subscribing to a newsletter. Remember, though, that online editions of the traditional media are usually cut-down versions of the original – they are useful for identifying the most important stories (often before they 'hit the streets') but they will not contain all of the information you will find in the original.

Do not forget, too, the growing source of news and local views published through 'citizen journalism'. Local blogs are harder to monitor. They come and go over time (often unannounced), and what is written will be of varying reliability too. Use websites that capture and aggregate blogs to help.

Remember other types of media too – local radio and TV for example will have relatively large audiences and will report on a wide range of local issues. All of these sources live on the pulse of the local community and your campaign should do so too.

CHAPTER 64

VIDEO

*The luminous screen in the home carries
fantastic authority.* Erik Barnouw

Got a website or a blog? Got a video camera, a phone or an iPad with a high-resolution video camera built in? Why not film yourself and bung it online? It is quick and easy and makes you look like you are down with the techno kids, doesn't it? Well, maybe – but there are plenty of reasons to be wary of DIY video production. You quickly discover why TV production specialists are paid a lot of money, and so too are good actors!

The challenges do not just affect amateur campaigners. Former British Prime Minister Gordon Brown's foray onto YouTube in April 2009 (http://www. youtube.com/watch?v=sBXj5l6ShpA) became a cult hit for the wrong reason: it was awful.

Part of the error was political – he rushed out a YouTube film in response to the developing political crisis over MPs' expenses and made commitments in the clip that he had not previously agreed with any of his colleagues. Scheduling time to produce online multimedia content is a good move, but what really matters is spending enough time on getting the contents of the announcement right. Substance matters.

What rubbed salt into the wounds of the colleagues who were not consulted was the other part of the error – Brown looked bad, with insincere smiles bursting out at all the wrong moments. Smiling when you are talking about a serious topic is not good. Smiling and looking like you are faking it is not good. Put the two together and you have a cult online hit.

At a technical level there was no problem: aspects such as the lighting, sound and focus were all done well (you need to bear these in mind if you produce your own material – invest in some good kit). It was the performer who did not perform.

One lesson from this is that you have to have someone slightly detached from the production process who can say, 'No, that isn't good enough.' We know a team that produced a YouTube clip which really wasn't good enough to go out, but everyone involved in the process got so sucked in to worrying about which take to use, when to release the film and so on that they lost sight of whether the quality was good enough overall. Never under-value someone with fresh eyes viewing the footage and giving their honest opinion.

A second lesson is to focus on the substance and the message. That means thinking about the right pictures as well as the right words. Do this in advance so you are not sucked into the details of getting the production right and end up producing something that is rotten at its core.

As you become more ambitious with the piece, the amount of effort required for professional sound and good-quality editing increases sharply. Far too many political clips fall into the netherworld of trying to be more ambitious than the simple talking head but do not have the necessary resources and skills to deploy the plan effectively. The result is a rather amateurish video. If all you can do well is simple, stick to simple and if you want and need something that is not simple, make sure the resources (money, time and equipment) and the skills of those involved (you may be able to get some very skilled people to donate their time – but make sure they really are very skilled) can cope.

There, we have got to the end without mentioning it is also a good idea not to appear online in your underwear...

CHAPTER 65

HIGH-VISIBILITY CAMPAIGNING

*The Invisible Man would have been a bad candidate
and an even worse campaign helper.*

Some parts of campaigning are all very modern and sophisticated. Narratives are crafted, social-media platforms are built, and audiences are segmented and targeted. Others are, frankly, more basic: you just need to let people know you are there.

Sometimes it just makes sense to have as many people as possible see that you are out campaigning. That might be because you are campaigning in an area previously neglected, and so you want people to see that things are changing, or because you want to show people your campaign has momentum and can win, or simply because you want people to start talking about you.

Here are some top tips to get the most from your efforts.

The first requirement of high-visibility campaigning is to pick a venue where many people can see you. Time as well as place matters – even the busiest of high streets is pretty quiet at 8 a.m. on a Sunday. An otherwise quiet backwater may be full of people when there is an event at the local stadium. Do your research, including inspecting venues at the right time of day and day of week. More than once, a debrief after a damp-squib event has included a comment from a well-meaning local activist along the lines of 'Yes, it's always quiet round here on a Saturday morning, I don't really know why...'

Make sure the right people are seeing you, too. Ed wasted a campaign Saturday at an obvious target for some 'hi-vis' campaigning: a large and busy supermarket. The candidate and the team were, indeed, busy all day. Shaking hands and talking to voters who could not vote for the candidate. The supermarket was the only one for miles around and on the rural edge of the constituency, which meant that barely any of the shoppers voted locally.

Make sure you have a good turnout of supporters. Nothing sells like success and a big crowd will look so much better than the candidate and a single bedraggled minder handing out limp leaflets on a damp Saturday morning on the high street. Make sure the candidate has a minder to ensure they do not spend all of their time talking to one person and to take notes of any useful information or points to follow up.

On the day, supporters should be highly visible – but not eccentric. Discourage the local activist who wants to cycle round the area with an improvised loud-hailer made from a rolled-up newspaper advertising the event. Yes, it has happened to us.

Supporters should act as a funnel for the candidate, making contact with the public and chanelling those interested towards the candidate. This optimises the candidate's time. Brief supporters to sign up voters to the campaign. And make sure you follow those contacts up!

Think carefully about campaign materials. Balloons,

badges and leaflets to hand out work well. One rather neat idea we observed was to give shoppers a carrier bag with the campaign material inside it. The bag was useful and the leaflets were likely to be read at home rather than dumped in the nearest bin.

A final tip – afterwards, make sure at least one person re-visits the places campaigned in to make sure discarded leaflets, lost balloons and the rest are all tidied up rather than left as an embarrassing reminder of who was there.

CHAPTER 66

PUBLIC MEETINGS

Always have more people than chairs – and remember,
you control the number of chairs.

Looking for a primer that will encourage your
team to get stuck into community campaigning? Annette Penhaligon's biography of her husband,
David, is an emotional read – the MP was killed in a
car accident at a time when many talked of him as
a potential leader of his party. His origins as a politician, though, lay deep in community campaigning.
Ed suggested that one candidate copy Penhaligon's
basic campaign blueprint of travelling from village
to village, setting up public meetings and recruiting
those who attended. This time, though, the effort fell
flat when the first meeting literally had an audience of
one (the guy had left his dog at home).

Times and politics have changed since David
Penhaligon was campaigning in the early 1970s but
that tough learning experience does not mean public
meetings no longer have a place in campaigning. It just
means you have to be smarter (than Ed was) at picking
the hook for the event, the venue and the speakers.

Public meetings can be a great way to demonstrate support for a cause, to motivate people, and to
exchange ideas and information. They are a tool
to be used sparingly, for it can be hard to get a good

attendance at a public meeting, but most campaigns fall into the mistake of using them too little rather than too much.

Picking a good venue makes a big difference. It should be easy to get to for the likely audience, and have both public and private transport options. It should be the right size – the ideal meeting has all the seats taken and a couple of people standing. Venues that are very flexible in the number of seats that are put out are hugely helpful in this respect, much more so than venues with seating attached to the floor. Republican Mitt Romney learned this lesson the hard way during the 2012 contest to be the presidential nominee when a big economic speech of his in Michigan fell completely flat: the crowd of 1,250 was housed in a stadium able to take 65,000. In a room designed for 1,200, 1,250 would have been a triumph; this was a disaster.

A good meeting chair makes a big difference. Chairing public meetings is a particular skill and though it can be tempting to have a 'big name' as the chair to attract the public, the priority should be to have a chair who will run things well. One of the speakers can be the name to help bring in the crowds.

Think carefully about the balance between speakers, and time for questions and answers. The more controversial the topic, the more people will be angered if they feel there is not plenty of question time.

Remember the impression the choice of speakers will give: are they all male or all from a variety of places or all officials? Make sure speakers know in advance how long they should talk for, can see a timepiece and have 'nearly-out-of-time' warnings when speaking. Glasses of water also help.

Advertise the meeting in advance thoroughly and encourage people to pass on information about it. Emails, tweets and other similar messages all should encourage people to pass on the news about the meeting. Always include an easy link to a map and transport information.

Have a sign-in sheet, and make sure it is passed around to everyone in the room. Ask for contact details so you can keep people informed about further news on the topic of the meeting. Leaflets on chairs are also a good way of getting more information to people and helping them remember who organised the meeting and how to get in touch.

In the digital age, meetings are making something of a comeback with high-profile candidates using 'town hall meet-ups' to put across their key campaign message. Using technology to bring that community event to a bigger audience makes sense, too.

Finally, make sure photographs – and videos – are taken of the meeting to use when you report to every-one interested in the issue how the meeting went and what the next steps are. This way you can keep in touch both with those who came to the meeting and with those interested in the subject but unable to make it.

The prologue and sequel to a meeting give it far more value than merely the meeting itself.

CHAPTER 67

LOBBYING

Ten people who speak make more noise than ten thousand who are silent. Napoleon Bonaparte

Sometimes in your campaigning, you need to persuade those already in power to do things, especially as you get active in single-issue campaigning (see Chapter 48). Successful lobbying combines skills that come naturally to a campaigner with some that do not.

The first step is to understand who does what in government. Make sure you know which group of people is responsible for the issue you are campaigning on, and be clear about who does what within that team (whether it is the public sector or the private sector). Who makes the decisions? Who advises the decision makers on what decisions they should make? In addition, exactly what decision do you want them to make?

In years gone by the web of influence was a difficult one to untangle. Increasingly, today, governments make information about roles and responsibilities publicly available. It will help to complete the picture if you can ask an expert, but a good deal of information about who does what in government is available online.

Take the time to understand the decision-making process. Where do political advisors and public servants fit in? Getting your message to them can often be more important than getting it directly to the busy politician who makes the final decision.

Look at when decisions are made. It will always be easier to get a decision in your favour before something is announced than to change a policy once it has been made. If your campaign requires a financial decision, is there a budgetary cycle you need to fit into? This applies as much to lobbying local government as it does central government, even if you are lobbying other organisations that you might be turning to for financial help (charities funding new play equipment for your community for example).

Look at what influences the people you need to influence; what sort of decisions they have favoured in the past and what arguments they like or recoil from. It is a rare issue that has only one attribute to it; understanding your targets lets you emphasise the most effective parts of it.

It will be easier to get a decision in your favour if your case matches the political priorities of the politicians. If they are looking to cut costs, can you demonstrate how your project will save public money? If they are interested in increasing participation, does it show how the people affected are involved in making decisions?

Then get the tone right. Angry and confrontational may be great for whipping up support from the public. It does rather less well for persuading the target of your ire to make the decisions you want. Instead, be constructive. Explain how your case fits with their priorities. Present a robust and detailed case, and explain how the changes you want to see can be delivered in practice.

Show also the breadth of public support for your requests. Petitions are an easy way to do this, but for that very reason usually often have only limited impact. Get supporters to write personal letters and to turn up to lobby people in person. Work with the politicians you are trying to influence rather than against them as far as you possibly can. If you need them to make a radical change in direction that they will not be comfortable with, then you need to gather the full force of public opinion on your side.

One final thought. All of the above is second nature to many party members who work in pressure group campaigning or public affairs, so you may well have skills among your supporters that are sat there waiting to be used.

CHAPTER 68

ADVERTISING

Advertising is only evil when it advertises evil things.
David Ogilvy

David Ogilvy, one of the creators and geniuses of the modern advertising industry, had a technique he called his secret weapon. He first used his secret weapon on the job that got him his big break – advertising a new hotel. What form did the weapon take? Five hundred postcards. Not the most glamorous or high-tech answer, you might think, but Ogilvy's secret weapon was direct advertising – sending the right message direct to the right people. Much of political campaigning is advertising, for door knocking, direct mail, emails and phone calls are all about taking the right message (hopefully) to the right people.

However, sometimes it is worth delving into the world of commercial advertising – whether it is through newspapers or, increasingly, advertising online, where Google and Facebook in particular provide many ways of cleverly targeting different audiences.

Online advertising is most obviously useful for reaching online audiences, but it is also a great way to test. Online adverts very rapidly generate data, particularly click rates that let you test out different designs and ideas. This sort of quick, relatively cheap, testing should be your norm.

People do not behave the same online as offline, but that sort of testing is often a useful guide for offline advertising, especially in campaigns where budgets are very tight. Which headline most grabs people's attention and so should be used on the front of a leaflet? Testing out different forms of wording with online adverts can help you work out the answer to that.

Remember Ogilvy's four pillars for advertising success when venturing into such territories:

- Research: you must understand the audience
- Professional discipline: skill is required...
- Creative brilliance: ... as is the spark of brilliance
- Results: do not forget the purpose of the adverts

That mix of skills rarely comes all in one person. Most often on political campaigns at least two people are needed – the methodical analyst and the inspirational creative. Money is often wasted when only part of the list of four is applied, such as getting excited by a clever creative idea but failing to measure whether or not it brings results.

Any successful campaign will have pillar one built in. It is almost impossible to win without understanding your audience. We cover numerous ways to gather information about your audience in other chapters of this book. Whether it is doorstep canvassing, surveys, campaign sign-ups (petition returns) or the demographics of your patch, all that data is pure gold to a professional advertising campaign. We hope we have made clear throughout that you should treat it that way, too.

Skill is learned. There are simple steps to follow that ensure a high-quality campaign. These include applying 'tricks of the trade' from advertising and sales good practice. They also include common-sense care in your preparations – whether it is sending yourself test emails before a mass mailout to check the formatting or making sure you don't refer to a village as a town in a direct mailshot (as one author confesses to doing one time).

Creative brilliance is harder to acquire (which is why ad agencies pay top dollar for it). Seek it out in your volunteer team or buy it in if you have to and you can afford it. Importantly, though, be prepared to listen to 'creatives' and understand what they are offering you – do not dismiss it as gimmickry (but be discerning, too).

Focusing on results is important because it is too easy to get wrapped up in the brilliance of a campaign that entertains and impresses but does not achieve the necessary political goals. Make sure you have a way of monitoring the impact of a campaign.

Paid-for advertising works if it is done properly. Often, to do it properly businesses have to pay a lot of money. It does not have to be a centrepiece of your campaign but if you decide to do it, do it right.

CHAPTER 69

PETITIONING WITH
A PURPOSE

*There is much more use for petitions than
as filler for the recycling bin.*

After the 2010 election, the UK government introduced a new online parliamentary petition system, where those that passed a high threshold for numbers of signatures might secure debating time in Parliament. The result? A mass of petitions from the serious to the silly, with many badly thought out, poorly spelled and remarkably myopic among them. Many campaigners have, however, taken to the system as online petitions require no more investment than a single mouse click from the signatory and the well organised can quickly gather thousands of signatures via new media networks.

Of course, the simplicity of the act – of signing a petition – is one of its greatest attractions. It is precisely why it remains a highly effective campaigning tool stretching back through history to at least pre-modern Imperial China, if not earlier. Big petitions (or smaller petitions that show there is big concern in a small community) will always have an impact. They do not guarantee a success – you will need many other campaigning skills alongside them to ensure that – but they are a great start, a great way to gauge and to show how much support there is for a cause.

They serve another purpose in your campaign, too. As well as helping you to gather support on a particular issue, they can feed into your own campaign by giving you information about local concerns and by allowing you to begin a dialogue with those signatories, which could end in them being active community champions and active members of your campaign team also.

When someone signs à petition they are saying, even if in a brief and passing way, 'I am concerned about this.' That should be the opening to a regular dialogue, giving them updates and finding out what they can do. Too often, however, a petition signature leads to nothing but silence (an automated follow-up sent out by someone's computer code excepted). Think of the last few petitions you signed and Google for further stories about them. Chances are the petition disappeared into a black hole with, if you are lucky, your petition signature eventually appearing in a list of signatures that was presented to someone, though even that is not always guaranteed.

In other words, petition signatures are too often treated with disrespect. The basics are easy, obviously – and all too often not done.

First, when someone signs a petition thank them – and ask them what further they can do to help the campaign. Online this is very easy with a follow-up email (remembering, of course, to have warned people that you would like to use their data this way). Offline, this more often means hand-delivering or posting thank-you letters. Either way, you should ask people to publicise the campaign further, such as by providing a handful of leaflets they can deliver to their neighbours.

Second, make sure the petition is presented – and report back to the signatories to tell them this has happened. The presentation makes for a great photo opportunity, with the photo then used in printed literature, online campaigning and presswork.

Third, keep in touch with the signatories after the presentation about the next steps in the campaign.

The third step, of course, requires a petition to be about more than just getting some signatures and instead to be part of a bigger campaign plan to deliver results on an issue, as we talked about in Chapter 48.

If it is not, you should not even put your own signature to it, let alone ask other people.

CHAPTER 70

DEMONSTRATIONS AND PRACTICAL ACTION

Don't just talk about problems; fix them.

Campaigning to win an election risks becoming a bit of a beef-burger production line. You concentrate on getting the right ingredients together in the right order, you cook it for the right length of time and slap it between two buns, give it to the customer and move on to the next one. Sometimes, though, a campaign can really come alive. Most often this happens when people get directly involved in a campaign to fix something that really matters to them. Then, you rise above the production line steps churning out leaflets, press releases, emails and the like, and instead your campaign really comes to life as people get enthused and involved.

Whether it is dressing up in Santa costumes with a group of disabled people to highlight access problems to Christmas shoppers (as Ed has done) or gathering support for your local library, a bit of imagination in your campaigning tactics goes a long way. Direct, practical action can take very simple forms, especially when parts of the target of your campaign are easy to fix directly.

Campaigning against graffiti in the local park playground? Failed to get the council to act? Nothing like some direct action with rubber gloves and water to provide both a direct improvement and a publicity hook to get further public and media interest.

The mayor of the Lithuanian capital Vilnius, Artūras Zuokas, took this a step further in 2011. He took photogenic direct action on the issue of illegally parked cars in his city by hiring a tank to drive over one such vehicle, crushing it in front of the massed ranks of the media with him prominently sat at the front of the tank. Unlike many other politicians who have flopped in similar military vehicle settings, such as Democrat presidential candidate Michael Dukakis, he wisely decided not to wear any sort of helmet.

(After the dust had settled, the story did not turn out quite so well in the end, as it came to light that the vehicle had been specially procured and placed for the incident, making it less direct action and more photo stunt.)

Even if there is no scope for dramatic direct action such as this, there often is scope for actions that gather further information. A favourite in many villages suffering from heavy traffic is the 'day of surveying' when a rota of people stand in protest with banners and count up the heavy lorries as they go past. It gives the campaign some profile and useful data to use in follow-up work.

Demonstrations also have their role, particularly if there is a meeting coming up at which a decision relevant to the campaign will be made. Remember that most people will see and hear of a demonstration via the media, so make plans accordingly – such as to demonstrate either in the daylight or under very good lighting, and with a start or end that involves a crowd of people and banners or props that make their purpose clear. Long marches are rarely a good idea – they take too long, people drift away and spread out, taking away the visual impact of people more closely batched together.

It is always worth bearing in mind the potential negatives from any direct-action campaign. If it is badly managed it could produce negative publicity. If you are seen to promise results that are not delivered then you risk acquiring more enemies than friends. And, if it is genuinely a community campaign rather than a partisan vehicle then you may find that politicians of other stripes are eager to participate and to take a share of the limelight.

One other, and – do not worry – almost always unnecessary, thought: make sure that if there is an issue on which feelings run high, care is taken to preserve the peace. Nothing serves your opponents quite so well as damage and disorder.

Direct action has the potential to add something of real value to your election campaign. It can galvanise activists. It can identify you with an issue that matters to voters in your area. Most of all, though, it is a route to achieving real change with and for the community – something that is of value whatever the outcome of the election.

CHAPTER 71

POSTER CAMPAIGNS

An empty window is a wasted window.

In Chapter 9 we explained why looking like a winner is so important. A strong poster display is a key part of that. This is not about the expensive (and of dubious impact) billboard posters that get plastered up on hoardings. It is about posters that your supporters put up on their own property.

Garden posters, window posters, drain-pipe posters: big, bold and simple. And lots of them. It matters because it shows everyone who passes that you have lots of support.

Use the pre-campaign period to gather pledges. You can use a simple pledge form where the voter consents to displaying the poster when the campaign comes round (and makes clear any special arrangements for displaying the board: 'don't squash the prize dahlias!') When your team puts up the posters, they should also pop a copy of the pledge form through the door with a thank-you note to remind the voter of their commitment.

Seek out poster sites on busy roads, bus routes, near polling stations and shopping areas. Be imaginative: in more than one campaign we have seen back gardens running alongside railway lines used as poster sites. Canal boats can be great poster sites, too, especially if moored next to a popular pub or restaurant.

Get your posters up early and seek out new poster sites in roads that already have a number on display. Remember, voters are more likely to make that public commitment if they see they are fitting in with their neighbours. It is also important to build commitments over a series of elections where possible. A big display of posters is habit forming.

Make sure the display is maintained. Like so many other aspects of a winning campaign, planning the logistics of a poster campaign is a big part of its success, including covering any repairs and replacing posters that go missing.

Recruit volunteers with suitable vehicles and suitable muscles to get the posters up. Give them a realistic number of sites to manage – if your territory is one hundred miles across a single person will not cope with the job!

Make it easy for voters to ask for a poster. Have a hotline number. Print the contact details in your campaign literature and display it prominently on your website. Include it in your direct mail and campaign emails. Let people request a poster by post, by phone, by email or by text message.

If the area you represent lacks gardens, make use of window stickers. This is harder because you are likely leaving the act of displaying the sticker (literally) in the hands of the voter. But if they do display the stickers you can still gain a sense of momentum. One candidate built up a strong personal following in his urban constituency. At election time you can see a number of tower blocks where a row of neighbours display window posters each spelling out a letter of his name, making a display with real impact.

If there is no tradition of posters in your area (yet!),

it may be hard going at first – and you will need to put time and effort into explaining to supporters why putting up a poster is worthwhile. Too many candidates assume that if they just dish out posters supporters will magically know why putting them up is important. They won't – you need to explain and educate.

However, once you do, it is well worth it – because posters make you look like a winner and that helps make you a winner too.

CHAPTER 72

FIND AND WORK WITH EXISTING GROUPS AND OPINION FORMERS

The individuals with whom we choose to discuss politics are the same people with whom we discuss other important matters in our lives.

In 2009, Oxford University Press published the results of research carried out by a trio of academics into how people talk about politics. What they found may sound unremarkable but it has profound implications on campaigning.

Their conclusion was that 'we do not consciously select specific individuals with whom to discuss politics. Instead, the individuals with whom we choose to discuss politics are the same people with whom we discuss other important matters in our lives.'

In other words, if you want to get your messages into the chatter among people – and you do, because word of mouth is so powerful – you cannot rely on people having special political conversations with 'outsiders'. You have to get into their existing networks and communities.

Some starting points for getting those entrances are obvious, such as the prominent people in local residents' associations, tenant groups, Neighbourhood Watches and other similar groups. Putting together a comprehensive list of such people is a must. Then, systematically reach out to them. Make sure you listen more than you talk and that you get a real understanding of the issues that concern them. Then take those issues and work out what you can do about them.

Local councils often have lists of local organisations that they use for consultations. Add to this information from local libraries and what you learn from local media. With some online research and asking your own supporters for details of local groups they know about, you should soon have a good list.

You need sensitive antennae. Community leaders can generate strong opinions both pro and anti that sometimes have no basis other than the views of an individual. Do not be turned off from making contact with an opinion leader because of one negative comment and do not lavish more attention than is warranted on someone because of a single endorsement.

Think, too, about the various local professions that are both opinion formers and chat often to residents, such as doctors, dentists and newsagents. Put together lists using the phone book, business directories and local knowledge.

The role of religious figures varies hugely between communities and religions, but in some places these should be a priority. Anyone involved with politics in England will be familiar with the notion that the Church of England is the 'Tory Party at prayer'. Nonsense, of course, but it is as much a reflection of the idea that the church *network* is one that has been exploited by Conservatives, just as Evangelical networks have been extremely useful to Republican candidates in the US and Catholic church networks were the basis of many right-of-centre European parties in the twentieth century.

Today the political and social dividing lines are more blurred than in the past, so those networks are much more open to politicians of a range of colours. Churches themselves have taken on active campaigning roles in relation to poverty in the developing world for example or environmental issues. Each of these is a potential connection for politicians who share their aims.

Finally, do not forget key figures in public life locally. Local councillors of your own party are likely to have well-developed networks of their own and many will be highly respected in their community. Tap into those networks (and respect the long-serving local representatives whose knowledge of their community will be extensive). At the most local level of government, councillors are often elected without a party label. Make sure you engage with them too even if they are not officially part of your team. They will be at the hub of an active network of contacts and their support will be of real value both in the election and in getting things done for the community.

Or in other words, think about who other people listen to and talk with, and tap into those networks to get your political messages out more widely.

CHAPTER 73

GET PLATFORMS FOR
YOURSELF

It's not a shrinking violet competition.

When we talk about platforms, we do not just mean taking to the boards at a meeting in a leaky village hall. It could be that, but we really mean a place from which to speak with authority. It might be on local radio or TV. It might be as a guest contributor to an online discussion or as an informed commentator in a local newspaper article.

The most effective way to give your candidate a platform is to create your own. Many of the tips in this book point you to ways of launching and running community campaigns. Each of those will give you an outlet for your candidate. You can, in part, create your own media by building up your own online audiences, especially via email lists (see Chapter 78).

The advantage of these platforms is that you are in control and you can use them to communicate the messages you want, bearing in mind always that they need to be interesting enough to retain or gain an audience. You lose some of that control when you make use of other people's platforms, such as speaking at the meeting of a neighbourhood organisation where you cannot set the agenda or choose the chair. The compensation for that loss of control is that you are using a platform that gets you to someone else's audience, beyond your own campaign's organic capabilities.

One candidate we worked with, for example, created her own public-transport lobby group, which brought people together to campaign on a key local issue.

You can put on public meetings about issues you are campaigning on, too (see Chapter 66). These campaigns also give you the scope to create a reputation (a positive one, as a local campaigner and a voice for local concerns). You can place yourself metaphorically at the centre of local conversations by providing the substance that people talk about, in particular with survey reports and research into local issues that you are campaigning on. If you are campaigning to re-generate a local high street, for example, producing 'the' statistic about the number of empty shops which everyone ends up citing not only makes the local discussions happen on terms friendly to your case, it also makes them happen around you.

Pretty soon you will find yourself being asked to speak in your own right because of your reputation as a campaigner.

Volunteer to help with campaigns in your community (if you agree with them!). Do not get lost in the back room, though. It is too tempting to accumulate committee positions that do little to further your campaign and that do much to eat up your precious time. By all means, find comrades to fill much-needed volunteer places in a local campaign – it will win you friends and help to keep you in touch with what is going on. But a long list of honorary treasurer positions will just mean too many evenings on the meeting circuit where you see the same half-dozen people over and over again.

Make sure the campaign organisers realise that your talents lie in acting as a spokesperson, in bringing a new audience to their campaign and in opening doors to decision makers.

If campaigners organise public platforms for their messages make sure you are involved. If it is a public meeting, for example, should you be one of the main speakers? If not, make sure you contribute from the floor with an intelligent question or useful comment.

Not just campaigns offer this outlet, remember. In an era of increasingly open and localised decision making by public bodies it is possible to get involved with a whole range of local bodies that provide a platform for your candidate and offer a source of real power, too. Again, do not overdo it. Only commit to involvement with organisations that you know you have the time and motivation to support properly.

You can enjoy the true delights of committee work once you have achieved your main goal and been elected.

CHAPTER 74

PLAN YOUR INTERNET CAMPAIGN

There is always more technology than time.

Voters find it surprising if a candidate is not online and candidates who do not make good use of the internet face losing out on votes, helpers and money. The internet has become an integral part of how elections are fought, so all elections are now internet elections.

Anglers use a saying: you need to fish where the fish are. The same applies to politics. You need to put out information, ask for money and look for helpers where the voters are. They are increasingly online, so campaigns need to be, too.

But you cannot simply put information online and then sit back and wait. Some people will come; far more will come if you also effectively promote it. That requires an understanding of who the audience is, or might be, for a candidate's online presence.

It usually has three key parts. Arguably the most important of the trio is the media, because if journalists pick up information online and then use that in their own stories, that information usually gets a much bigger audience than the original online audience.

Just look at the number of views that local candidate

films on YouTube receive in the UK. It is a rare clip that gets more than 1,000 views, but it is a rare local paper that has fewer than 1,000 readers.

Another part of the audience is the internal audience. Whether it is councillors, activists, members, helpers or donors, they all need to be kept happy and motivated. The online world offers many opportunities to do just that, and to turn that extra enthusiasm into extra offline campaigning. This was the big success of the Barack Obama 2008 internet campaign. It mobilised people online to give money (largely spent on TV adverts in the offline world) and to go and knock on doors, make phone calls and deliver leaflets (all also aimed at the offline world).

The final part of the audience comprises the floating voters. The media and the internal audience are ways to get at floating voters too, but there is also a direct online audience. It is rarely a large enough audience in itself to allow you to neglect the offline world, but already candidates find their direct online audience now reaches more people than the local newspapers in their constituency.

It is easy to get lost in the blizzard of different online services: websites, blogs, Twitter, instant messaging, email, Facebook, YouTube, Instagram and more. Not even Barack Obama's massive team effectively made use of them all. (Look at his Twitter account during the election campaign for an example of boring, non-interactive minimalism.)

The best starting place is with a blank sheet of paper and three rows: 'media', 'internal audience' and 'floating voters'. Write in each row the key pieces of information that they want or that you want them to have.

There will usually be a large overlap between what a candidate wants people to know and what people actually want to know, but a candidate should aim to do more than just simply provide people with the information they already think they want.

As a final piece of preparation, take a look around the existing online presence from all political parties, the council, the local media and other local news sources (such as bloggers and local organisations). This may highlight gaps in the provision of local information that a candidate can usefully fill.

Armed with your basic sketch of the audience, the information to supply and the gaps in the information already out there (which professionals in this field may recognise as a hugely simplified version of the persona and information architecture processes they commonly use), good decisions can be made about what online presence to build.

CHAPTER 75

ONLINE AUDIENCES TAKE TIME TO BUILD

It is the tortoise and not the hare that
wins in online campaigning.

Online marketing pioneer American David Meerman Scott wrote a blog post in 2011 titled 'The secret to getting 50,000 followers on Twitter'.

His secret applies just as well – if not, in fact, even better – to the world of politics, and not only to getting a large number of Twitter followers but also to getting a large number of email subscribers, Facebook fans, blog readers or any other online audience.

The secret? As Meerman Scott put it, based on music industry marketing advice he heard, 'The secret is that there is no secret … You need to build a fan base one effort at a time over the long haul.'

The fast-moving story that sweeps around the world may catch the headlines, but the reality of most internet campaigning is very different: it is the gradual, consistent and sustained effort that reaps the reward. Unless you are very lucky, it is a commitment to building up email lists, web visitors and so on over time that brings results.

Gradual steady progress still has to be fast enough to get you to your goal. Take, as an example, a councillor up for election in twelve months who is starting with an email list of zero. If they add on average one email address a day to their list, by the time the election starts that will give an email list of around 350, allowing for a little drop-off as people move, unsubscribe and so on. If they need 1,000 votes to win, then that is a big enough list to have a major impact. If they are in a large urban ward and looking at 3,000 or so votes, that 350 list looks rather too small, and even if they are in a smaller ward if their email address growth rate is but one a week, that is going to be of little use other than in an ultra-marginal knife-edge contest.

The same applies in other parts of the online world. Google, for example, likes to give prominence to sites which have been around for a while and are regularly updated (rather than being quickly produced spammy sites), so regular production of new content gradually makes your site perform better in search engines over time. Facebook places a great premium on people interacting with your content; the more people who do, the more visible your content is made to others. You therefore need to get into that virtuous circle of more people interacting so more people see your content so more people are interacting...

None of this should be taken as an endorsement for taking it easy. You will grow your audience if you work hard at it over a continuous period. That means producing regular outputs that people will want to read and chasing sign-ups wherever you can find them. But do not plan on taking over the virtual world overnight as an easy route to winning your campaign.

So, work out what the slow but steady rate is which gets to a useful destination, and then get to work.

CHAPTER 76

WEBSITE, BLOG OR SOMETHING ELSE?

It is not what you can start that matters,
it is what you can maintain.

Armed with your basic sketch of the audience, the information to supply and the gaps in the information already out there, good decisions can be made about what online presence to build.

At the heart of it needs to be a web page of some sort. It could be a website, a blog or a combination of the two. The death of websites is already being pronounced in some quarters but don't believe it — there is still a need for sites showing information that a wide range of visitors might search for.

Blogs often suit the personal tone of voice, which is great for conveying conviction, beliefs and sincerity.

In addition, blogs are to websites as newspapers are to books. They are best suited for regular updates, often briefer stories and building an audience which expects a new edition most days.

That all means blogs require a regular, personal contribution from someone who can write well. Websites that are more traditional are more suited to those with a standard writing style or with less time or news to impart. A website needs regular updating, but to get the most out of a blog its minimum frequency of updating is far higher than for a website.

It is a matter of juggling skills, priorities and resources. Some candidates end up with both a website and a blog, but this rarely works effectively (two different sites to look after, too fragmented an online presence) unless they are closely integrated or it is a big campaign with a big team and internet presence.

Some of the basics to make sure you include on your site, whether it is a blog or website, are:

- Email sign-up box (see Chapter 78 on the importance of emails)
- Ability for people to volunteer
- Latest news about your campaigns
- Links to other local sites from your party, councillors and the national/regional party sites
- Election imprint and data protection disclaimer
- RSS (or news feeds) – these provide an easy way for people to sign up to receive new content automatically in future. Any decent website or blog system will provide RSS options
- Options to promote your presence on social networks (where appropriate) and to share content from the site via them.

Photographs and headlines also matter. People skim-read online just as they do offline. Photographs catch the eye even when the carefully nuanced sub-clause is not read.

Good action photographs are vital. The photographs should illustrate the main messages overall, present the candidate in a positive light and obey the law of the left nostril (see Chapter 58).

That sounds obvious, but if you take a quick browse around some candidate websites or blogs, you will see that far too often the photo of the candidate looks more like something out of a regional news crime report than an image conveying a positive message. A candidate claiming widespread popular support does themselves no favours being photographed on their own all the time. (And do not think you can get away with using a member of staff to be the public in a photograph, as British Conservative candidate Jacob Rees-Mogg found to his cost with a lengthy exposé in the *Daily Mail*.)

Powerful headlines that attract attention are important. People viewing links to your sites or with an RSS feed will see the headlines first. Without a good headline, they may never come to the site to read the full story. Pay attention to some commonsense aspects of design.

CHAPTER 77

PROMOTING YOUR
SITE ONLINE

Online campaigns are like a baby. Getting them to be
live is your pregnancy and then you launch them – and
that's birth – and then they keep you up at night and
cost you more than you think and you need to look after
them all the time because if you don't they die.
Anna Rafferty, Penguin Books

Simply being online is not enough. There are plenty of dead websites, unloved email lists, derelict Facebook pages and the like. Once you are online, you need to keep working.

Although the single most important step in getting people interested in what you are doing online is providing good-quality content, that is not enough on its own. People base whole careers and businesses on promoting websites and blogs, but there are many simple steps a candidate can take to promote their website, blog or indeed profiles on social networks.

Leaflets are an excellent place to start. Do not just stick the address on a leaflet; include stories which give people a positive reason to visit a site online. For example, a story about school admission rules might include a link to further details. A good tip when giving web or blog addresses (URLs) is to capitalise words as this makes them easier to read, remember and type – www.MarkPack.org.uk rather than www.markpack.org.uk. Both will end up at the same website.

Alongside printed communications, verbal promotion has a useful role to play. Whether it is canvassing, meeting voters in the high street, visiting groups or making speeches, most candidates will find plenty of opportunities to mention their web address. Ensure, therefore, that your web address is easy to say! Also, grab the web addresses that cover obvious mistakes and mishearings, and point them at your site, too.

Then there is the media. The days when simply launching a website made for a news story are mostly gone, but with a little imagination stories can often be generated. For example, launching an online survey can be a great way of getting your web address in the newspapers. Remember your internal audience and look for publicity on other sites that they read.

But overall, email is so important that we would rather run an election campaign in which the website and blog failed than one in which the email setup failed. Nearly nine in ten UK internet users are on email. That is far more than visit blogs or political websites. Gather up email addresses (with consent to use them) from members, local journalists and voters, then use them to let people know when significant new content has been added. You can also use other online channels, such as your own profiles on social networks – and contact your supporters to encourage them to do likewise.

You can also get people to send information around online for you, if you make your content shareable, for increasingly people read content online after a recommendation. At a technical level you can assist this by having 'share this' type buttons on content, such as to send a post to Twitter or Facebook. It is also about content: think about what content your audiences might want to share with others. Only the very best political rants (or the very worst!) are shared. Useful local information is usually a much stronger bet.

Finally, watch out for good opportunities to comment on other sites. Many websites and blogs take comments and this is a good way of taking part in the conversation where the audience already is. It is also likely to expose you to conflicting views from others, which is a useful check against falling into the myopic mindset about how your party is fantastic and everyone in other parties is the spawn of the devil.

Above all, remember the quote we started this section with – promotion is not a one-off act, it is a continuing nurturing and building of the online profile, week in and week out.

CHAPTER 78

EMAIL CAMPAIGNING

Many of your voters are younger than email.
Isn't it time you started using it?

Email matters. It is the oldest, and still often the most effective, online campaigning tool. It does not get the same glitzy attention as whatever the newest, latest technology does but smart internet campaigners know that a well-run email list lies at the heart of successful online political campaigns.

Email is powerful because it lets you push out messages when you want to (unlike, say, a website, which relies on people coming to you when they want to); it lets you divide the audience into different segments to receive different messages at different times (very hard to do with, for example, Twitter); and it is a good driver of traffic to other online activities.

It also adds speed, convenience and topicality to the armoury of more traditional campaigning techniques. So it means you can reach hundreds of people with your message quickly even in rural areas or in bad weather. It can help you build a sense of momentum and urgency to your campaign – letting people know straightaway about an important decision affecting their community; about a fundraising target being met or about a candidate being chosen to trigger the start of a campaign.

All of those benefits require you to have a decent number of email addresses, and it takes time to build up a good list. So start early and widely advertise the ability for people to join your email list – not only via the website and social media, but also in printed literature, in sign-up forms passed around at events and when your team are talking to the public on the phone or on doorsteps.

Once you have someone on an email list, you need to keep them. Too many emails can put people off but (as with leaflets through the letterbox) complaints about too many usually really mean that they are not interesting enough. If people are really interested, they will happily receive large volumes of communication. A good test for each email is to check whether a recipient can work out the answer to the question 'Why have I been sent this email and why now?' Timely information about changes to local bus services passes that test; a long screed of policy does not.

The three numbers a campaign should keep careful track of are the number of people on the email list, the open rate and the click-through rate.

Email open-rate statistics are provided by most of the email-management services available, and indeed they are one of the main reasons for using such a service (along with the fact that the good ones sort out all the complicated technical work for you and also make it easy to send emails in both HTML and plain-text versions).

Knowing roughly how many people open each of your emails is rather like knowing how many people return a residents' survey. If you know the number you can experiment with the design, content and timing (very important as readership varies greatly depending on whether you send the email at a good or bad time) to see what gets the best response. If you do not know the number, you are working blind and almost certainly not getting the most out of your communications.

Some people like also keeping an eye on the unsubscribe rate, and there is no harm in doing so, although in our experience it does not add to what you learn from the open rate.

What does is the click-through rate. Knowing how many people click on the links in your email and which links they click on again is crucial to being able to produce emails that work effectively.

It is all too easy to think that hitting 'send' on lots of emails means job done. It is only job done if they are read and acted on.

CHAPTER 79

ONLINE POLITICAL ACTIVITY IS ONLINE PERSONAL ACTIVITY

The personal is political.

Every feminist will tell you that the personal is political. When the phrase was first coined, it is unlikely that its authors had in mind the internet but the online world has brought the personal and the political together like never before.

Pioneering feminists meant that personal acts could be a powerful tool for political change. That is potentially true of the internet, too, of course – social media played an important part in the Arab Spring of 2011.

But it brings with it a whole other meaning. In a world where we have grown used to sharing our thoughts instantly via Facebook or Twitter a danger exists in sharing too much. Use the internet wisely and think carefully about the boundaries between the personal and the public sphere.

Particularly since the rise of social media, the most effective approach to using the internet for political campaigning is a personal one, that is, presenting a human face rather than an impersonal organisational face.

You see that most clearly on Twitter: only the rare

impersonal, third-person tone of voice account does well, unless it is simply pumping out the headlines for an already popular website. Instead, it is the human touch that works.

That can be risky, as exposing a personal face to the world requires the personal face to be presentable. As someone once quipped about US Republican Senator Chuck Grassley and his opponent, 'As long as he has a Twitter feed, she has a chance.' Numerous candidates have been tripped up as the online world reveals them to be stupid, rude, arrogant, bigoted or all four. But the personal touch is still the one to aim for.

The same is true in different ways in other online mediums, even when the technology choices may sometimes apparently point towards the less personal approach. So on Facebook, for example, there is much merit in using a page rather than a personal profile, but pages work best for candidates when they are built very much around them and run in a human, interactive way.

This applies to multimedia as well as written online content. Take a look at the photographs used, for example: do they feature you heavily or are they impersonal photographs? It applies to the style of writing most obviously. Even a non-blog website can come over as being from an interesting human or from an impersonal organisation, depending on the choice of photographs and the tone of the writing.

It also applies to responding to interactions online. It is inevitable you will come across the rude, the eccentric and apparently mad. However, if you insist on avoiding such people you need not only turn off your computer, you need also lock yourself in a room and take the phone off the hook. You perhaps also should therefore not be a candidate (even if this novel communications approach may be worth a newspaper story or two).

Do respond. There is nothing worse than leaving an impression of arrogant disregard for people's views by doing something online and then ignoring the reactions it causes. Moreover, as online mechanisms do tend to bring out the more acerbic traits in people it is always worth being polite back to someone once to see how that works.

That leaves a tricky balance for most campaigns: how much does the candidate do personally and how much does someone do for them? Two golden rules are in tension. Do not pretend that someone is doing something when someone else is pressing the keys; devolve and build a bigger team, for the candidate cannot do everything.

Wherever the balance lies best for your campaign, make sure the personality of the candidate whose name is on the ballot paper comes through strongly and clearly.

CHAPTER 80

LISTEN ONLINE AND OFFLINE

*Bore, n.: A person who talks when you
wish him to listen.* Ambrose Bierce

STOP TALKING FOR A MINUTE AND LISTEN!

We know it is not easy. If we did not think we had so many great ideas about election campaigning we would have just sold you a blank book and asked you to write in yours.

One of the most valuable skills a politician can learn is the importance of listening.

Poke around on the internet for a while and you will find all sorts of information about how we communicate with each other. How we think the best conversations are the ones where we do all the talking. How most of the time when the other person is talking we are not listening but actually thinking about what we are going to say next.

Candidates often feel that they are bursting with good ideas and even better intentions which they just want to tell the world about. Yet often what the public wants is to be listened to and, just as in non-political settings, closing your mouth and listening is often the way to impress people with your wisdom and sagacity. The more someone listens, the better other people think of them – not only as a listener but also numerous other ways.

There is another reason for listening when being a politician. The public gets the final say in the ballot box, so knowing what people are thinking is critically important. A skilled leader can shape as well as follow opinion; but you can only shape that which you know – so listen first.

We believe in practising what we preach, so this chapter is deliberately short. Use the time we have saved you by picking up the phone to two friends and asking them for their best piece of advice for you.

CHAPTER 81

THE POWER OF WORD
OF MOUTH

Electric communication will never be a substitute for
the face of someone who with their soul encourages
another person to be brave and true. Charles Dickens

Political scientists and campaigners poring over
the details of Labour's landslide 1997 general
election result were at first faced with a puzzle. Labour
appeared to have had an extremely effective election
machine, yet looking at the swings in its target seats
where it had poured in extra resources, they were no
higher than in many other non-target seats. How did
Labour manage to win so handsomely with such an
apparently skilful operation while also failing to gain
an extra edge in the marginals?

The answer came with survey data that showed
what the public got up to during the election. So
many people were enthusiastic at the thought of Tony
Blair winning and ousting the Tories (this was 1997)
that they eagerly talked to – and persuaded – other
people they knew, went out of their way to put up
posters, volunteered to campaign and so on. This
surge of activism and word of mouth spread across the
country, dampening out the campaign edge we would
have otherwise seen in the marginal seats.

This power of word of mouth comes from the adage

that, as the geographers Johnston and Pattie put it in their *Putting Voters in Their Place*, 'People who talk together, vote together.'

A campaign can encourage word of mouth on its behalf by making it easier for the public to express its views in public and to pass on those views.

Making it easy includes steps covered in previous chapters: provide window posters for campaigns; supply information on how to write to the local papers or take part in phone-ins; send people emails designed to entice readers to forward them; provide people with flyers, petitions or surveys to pass on to neighbours; and make use of online options where appropriate.

Good sound bites and pithy facts help fuel those conversations others can have on your behalf. Campaigns now often provide their own supporters with 'key talking points'. These work best when they are simple, easy to remember and not too politically obsessed; in other words, the sort of thing you might say in passing while chatting to your neighbour rather than the sort of thing reserved for politics essays.

Another effective approach is to make sure you talk to people who talk to people. Taxi drivers, hairdressers, shopkeepers. They are voters in their own right, of course, and they have concerns that deserve to be addressed, issues that affect their own business, for example. All the same rules about being a good campaigner – and a good representative – apply here. If you choose to campaign on an issue do so because it is in line with your beliefs, not because it appeals to a convenient interest group. Be sincere and follow the campaign through to a conclusion.

Resources invested in reaching out to 'opinion

formers' could well be repaid by those people becoming effective advocates for your campaign. There are other groups in this category too – religious leaders or people who run community groups, for example. And while public servants, rightly, shy away from acting as political advocates you should be aware that public places where people gather are places where you can campaign effectively with the crowd, such as at the local library on an issue which concerns parents or older people.

Word of mouth is a powerful medium that can be used by your campaign to great effect.

But as advertising expert Jef Richards says, 'While it may be true that the best advertising is word of mouth, never lose sight of the fact it also can be the worst advertising.' If you mess up, word of mouth can be used just as powerfully against you.

CHAPTER 82

DON'T DISS THE BRAND

*To all intents and purposes, Western philosophy began
with the ancient Greeks. So too did branding.*
Thom Braun

Here is a simple, fun game to play. Find a colour
picture of the McDonald's logo, the golden
arches. Cover all but the top quarter of just one of
the arches and show it to a number of people, asking
them if they know what it is. It is our bet that the vast
majority of them will correctly identify it even though
they see only a fraction of the image (an image of a
company logo, remember, which in itself is no more than
a picture). Try it again with the end of the Coke 'swirl'.

So much has been invested in establishing those
commercial brands that seeing a tiny part of the logo
allows potential customers to understand what they
represent. And that representation goes far beyond
simply knowing the name of the store or product. A
successful brand carries with it a whole set of values,
emotions and information in a single shortcut.

And that is just what candidates need. In fact, they
need it even more than commercial brands, as most
members of the public will happily spend more time
debating the relative virtues of different hamburg-
ers and vegetarian alternatives than thinking of the
choices between different candidates.

Good branding, in both the commercial and the political worlds, starts with a respect for the audience, a desire to understand it and a hunger to meet its needs.

We do not advocate market-testing your principles to see which ones you should change to attract more custom. But we do advocate learning some of the most important lessons from professional marketers when it comes to getting your message across.

When it comes to branding, those lessons are simple and valuable.

The first lesson is that if you have an established brand, use it. Most obviously, this will apply to candidates standing for a political party. Modern political parties invest heavily in developing their branding. So, use the party logo and colour scheme for example, rather than insisting on developing your own. The strongest brand identifier for a political party will usually be the party leader. So make use of their name and image in your campaign (unless the party leader is so unpopular that even the party itself has stopped mentioning them).

As far as possible, choose messages that run with the groove of the party's image. A successful brand will create a distinctive identity for the party (and thus for your campaign). A successful brand will suggest that the product – the political party – is relevant and is of a high quality. Branding creates those shortcuts for the voter that means that you can make it do some of your campaigning work for you.

Do not undermine the brand carelessly. Whether it is your own image or that of your party, think carefully about how your actions and words will be perceived in relation to that image. There are plenty of examples of how a single lapse of judgement can bring a carefully built-up image crashing down in an instant.

The central message of this book is that your own leadership and activism can change the result of an election. So do not simply rely on your established image (or that of your party) to carry you through. Equally, do not despair if your party's brand is temporarily damaged.

Despite all of that, remember that the brand cannot do everything for you. Use the resources you have available to make your campaign work as efficiently as possible but make sure it works as hard as possible, too.

CHAPTER 83

DEALING WITH
CORRESPONDENCE

*What is written without effort is, in general,
read without pleasure.* Samuel Johnson

The public is less engaged with politics than ever
before. We know this because fewer people
vote, fewer people get involved with political parties
and fewer people consume political news. That is the
standard theory at least, but there is one area where
voters are defying the convention: more and more
of them are willing to write to their representatives
about issues that concern them.

You should welcome this and make it easy for people
to write to you. Publicise contact details prominently
and give voters a number of different ways to get in
touch: by email, by text, by old-fashioned 'snail mail'.

There are four important tips to keep in mind when
it comes to correspondence with voters.

The first is to deal with each contact properly. Make
sure that people receive a prompt, polite reply that
addresses their concern and contains an indication
of the action that you will take. If your campaign
is dealing with large volumes of correspondence
it is common to send out holding replies at first.
There is nothing wrong with this since it will, at least,
confirm that you have received the letter or email. But

remember that the voter will recognise it for what it is; they will still want a 'proper' reply as quickly as possible.

Do think before you write – do not reply in anger even if the contact you receive is abusive. Always ask yourself, how would your reply look if it found its way to a journalist? It is also worth remembering that even someone who is initially rude will often (if not always!) be polite next time round – once their moment of anger has passed and your reply has mollified them. There are some people who are persistently abusive but, in our experience, nine out of ten rude people turn out to be perfectly decent once you give them a second chance.

One candidate we know got into the habit of telephoning correspondents to reply to letters. This can work if you are dealing with a small volume of correspondence as it adds a particularly personal touch. But it does not always work – if the voter was writing to let off steam they might have chosen to write precisely because they did not want to speak to you. Phone calls also mean you do not have such good records about who said what and the details of information mentioned.

The second tip is to make sure you have a system in place to cope with the correspondence. This will be particularly important at critical points where your profile changes, such as when the official campaign begins or after you win. The volume of correspondence can increase dramatically at these points and you need to be ready to cope. Otherwise you will find yourself fighting a backlog and either losing votes because of the backlog or losing votes because you have to sacrifice other priorities to deal with it.

If you are running for a political party you may find they have bespoke software that helps you to manage correspondence. If not, there are plenty of options for correspondence management systems, which you can buy off the shelf. Assess how much time it will take to manage correspondence (even with the right software) and whether that means recruiting staff to deal with it.

The third tip is to listen carefully to what the correspondence is telling you. It is important not to over-react. If two or three people write to tell you that you are an idiot, well, it may just be that they always felt that way. If two or three hundred people write to tell you that you are wrong on an issue then it is wise to take particular note. But it is not just about volume. Some very large write-in campaigns can be organised using online 'one click' email campaigns but some very important (often local) issues might be raised by only a handful of people.

Our fourth tip is to make full use of the campaigning opportunity that an issue gives you. A personal issue raised by a voter is confidential and dealt with that way. But if a voter writes to tell you about an issue that affects a whole street, such as over-running road works, you should tell the whole street when you get the problem fixed. And if a campaign is needed to get a problem fixed remember to ask the correspondent to help with that campaign by taking a petition to their neighbours or delivering leaflets to them or organising a meeting in their neighbourhood.

The dialogue you build up directly with individuals will be invaluable to your campaign. And it is good for democracy, too. Make full use of it and you will run a better campaign and be a better representative.

CHAPTER 84

COMMUNICATE ALL
YEAR ROUND

*Politics is more dangerous than war, for in war you
are only killed once.* Winston Churchill

Back in the 1970s a new class of political activists appeared. Young, radical and disillusioned,
many of them rejected 'traditional' party politics all
together. Instead, they opted for direct action on the
issues that mattered to them. Yet some of those techniques did seep into mainstream party politics because
they offered a way to address a real weakness in the
party political system. Machine politicians seemed
to have become disconnected from an electorate
that was increasingly unwilling to play a passive part
in government.

In British politics, the then Liberal Party made
rather a cliché out of the slogan 'Working for you all
year round – not just at election time'. So potent was
its message that other parties have taken to copying
it, with a varying degree of re-wording depending on
how shameless a particular campaign feels (and there
was always plenty of amusement to be had from the
campaign that said how horrible the Liberals were
while also lifting campaign slogans and tactics for
their own use).

There are four reasons why the idea is a potent one.

First, the public may not pay much attention to politics outside of election time normally, but the public also wants to know that politicians are taking action on the big issues in between election times. A voter may not be that interested in a particular party's health policies outside of election time but they do want to know that the party is still caring about trying to get the health system right in between elections and is there ready and willing to help whenever a new or individual issue comes up.

This is why research by MORI into what people expect of their local government councillors found holding regular surgeries where people can go and raise issues came out very highly – even though very few people ever go to such surgeries. Knowing councillors are willing to listen all year round is reassuring, even if you do not have anything you want to go and say to them.

Second, the public likes people who will work hard on their behalf – and why not? Politicians might feel aggrieved at being accused of being lazy if they are locked for hours on end in committee meetings, but increasingly that is seen as only part of a politician's role. Campaigning all year is a good indicator that someone is really a hard worker.

Third, as we've touched on in other sections, the public doesn't pay that much attention to political campaigning – so you need to campaign all year round in order to have a chance of getting cumulative attention from people. It is a slightly demoralising thought but nonetheless true – you really do have to work harder just to get your message across between the reality shows on TV and the pizza leaflets on the doormat.

There is also a fourth reason why campaigning and communicating all year is worth doing, even if none of the first three applied. It is the right thing to do. Politicians and political institutions exercise power day in, day out, which affects people's lives. Even at 2 a.m. on a Sunday, the decisions made previously about police resources affect what happens when someone reports a burglary.

Good campaigners and good politicians are trying to influence decisions all year round – and to do that well you need to be listening to what the public's experiences are and roping in the public to help you have an impact. You cannot just disappear off the public radar in between elections if you want to be a good politician, let alone a successful one.

CHAPTER 85

TREAT PEOPLE
AS INDIVIDUALS

*While the people who hated me preyed on my mind,
they didn't take up my time. That was left to
the people who liked me.* Oona King

Other than in elections with the very smallest of electorates, it can be tempting to lose sight of individuals and slip into thinking of the electorate as statistics rather than a collection of distinct human beings.

It is a natural and even sometimes necessary reaction to fighting an election on the requisite scale to win but it is not practical to send a different, handcrafted letter to each voter. Some degree of aggregation is necessary.

But aggregation must be kept to a minimum. Within a consistent message, you should be picking the aspects that are of most interest to particular people and presenting those via the communications channels that best suit.

The sort of micro-targeting – given a fashionable twist and profile by the Republican and then Democratic presidential campaigns of the early twenty-first century but used decades previously in other countries such as Israel – works best when you remember to say the right thing to the right person, not different things to different people.

Such targeting does not mean saying one thing to one person and the opposite to another. It means saying the right things to the right people. To take a simple example, often young voters will have different policy interests from older voters. Young voters are less likely to be interested in your position on pensions or health care than are older voters. Younger voters might be more interested in your policies on public transport, say. There will be overlaps, of course: higher-education policy interests students and their parents. But focusing on different issues in, say, letters to individual voters does not mean you should tell them contradictory things – if you do you will be caught out, and rightly so, when they do talk.

How far you go in dividing up your electorate into finer and finer segments depends on a number of things. To be done effectively, though, micro-targeting requires a good accumulation of data (see Chapters 34–37) and its application to communication methods that allow for easy variations. Direct mail, email and online adverts are particularly good for this targeted variation in messages between different voters.

Online, in particular, it can be tempting to lose yourself in the data and the possibilities of variation. Always retain a sense check – if the groups end up too tiny, the time put into coming up with yet another different message for them is unlikely to be time well spent unless the tiny group has a particularly high value.

One example of successfully targeting a small group of voters comes from one of your authors in a British general election. A special mailing for one target constituency sent to its overseas voters could never win that many voters. There were not enough of them. But it was easy to do, requiring only some small changes to another target mailing, and brought in enough donations not only to pay for itself but also fund extra campaigning aimed at other voters.

By contrast, a different effort in a different election at targeting the four farmers in an otherwise urban constituency was a waste of time as they did not even have fields in useful places to display posters. It was the wrong group to spend time and effort on getting a special message to.

Do not make the same mistake – but do vary the message to meet different people's interests.

CHAPTER 86

MAKE SURE YOUR
SUPPORTERS CAN VOTE

To vote for you, someone has to be able to vote.

The most amazingly persuasive of messages delivered in the most effective and timely way are of no use if the successfully persuaded person is not actually able to vote. Traditionally in the UK, very high electoral registration rates secured by the official registration work by local councils have meant that political parties and candidates need to do little to help people register. However, the UK is becoming more like countries such as the US, where parties and candidates can help with registration – the official processes do not catch everyone.

There are two prime reasons for this change in the UK. First, increasing population movements, especially in urban areas, mean people may well have moved between registration and election but not have updated their register entry with their new address. Second, the UK is moving towards a system of individual electoral registration, where each person has to register personally – and provide more personal information than in the past – rather than just the one person in a household being able to register the whole household. That will particularly have an impact in places such as universities where the university administration have traditionally registered in one go all the relevant people staying in halls of residence and will no longer be able to do so.

People who are not registered, you might be surprised to know, are often very willing to vote if someone helps them out to get registered. That has often been the experience with registration campaigns in the US, for example, where voting rates among those pushed to register are often comparable to voting rates among those who get registered of their own volition.

It is not that people do not register because they have no interest in voting – well, some do but not all by any means. Rather it is practical issues, like having just moved or mislaid the form or not quite got round to filling out the form, which keep people off the register. Help sort that out for them and they may well vote.

In some areas, it is possible to identify neighbourhoods with a rapid turnover of voters (which thus risk having a higher rate of non-registration). Areas with large numbers of students, for example, are easy to target because not only do the 'student houses' tend to be clustered together but they also all move in at the same time of year. An autumn canvass of these neighbourhoods can be a useful way of reaching out to a whole bunch of new voters whether they are on the register or not. In other areas with more settled populations we have known particularly diligent campaigners keep track of houses with estate agent (realtor) boards outside properties so that they can make contact with the new residents when they move in.

There is a three-part process to getting supporters registered: let people know how they can check if they are on the register, tell them how to get registered and give them a good reason to do so.

In areas of particularly strong support, campaigns sometimes target properties that are known not to be on the electoral register, telling the occupants this. Otherwise, people going out door knocking should always be on the lookout for possibly unregistered people and the registration message can be pushed strongly in communications.

Aside from being registered to vote, people need to be able to get to their polling station. If voters finds it difficult to get to vote – or think they may not find the time to go and vote – prompt them to sign up for a postal or proxy vote (or, where it is allowed, to vote early in advance of polling day). Ask known supporters in good time and make it easy for them to do so by providing copies of the relevant forms for them to fill in.

Then, finally, there is the simple step of persuading people to cast their vote, which is the subject of Chapter 87.

CHAPTER 87

GET OUT THE VOTE (GOTV)

Answer three questions to get one vote.

For a large but shrinking number of voters, voting is a habit and something they will do without any encouragement or information from election campaigns. However, for many people what campaigns do or do not do to get out their vote makes the difference between voting and not. The hard core of determined and decided non-voters are joined each election time by the much larger ranks of the 'did not quite get round to it' people.

To get such people out to vote you need to answer three questions for them: Will my vote make a difference? How will the result matter to me? How do I vote?

The answer to the first question can take two forms. The more conventional is that the election is close and every vote will count. That is not always a convincing argument, but it can be supplemented by the argument that each vote will help send a powerful message. If your campaign is based on saving a local public service, for example, it is not just winning that boosts the campaign, it is the margin of victory – every vote adds an extra weight to the campaign.

Linking the result to someone's own priorities answers the second. Simply knowing that an election is close and a vote may nudge one politician ahead of another is not reason enough. Why should the person care which of the politicians wins?

Finally let know someone how to vote. In one successful campaign, the authors were part of a community which did not receive its official notice of where the polling station was located. The campaign produced and delivered a leaflet at the last minute that not only told them where to vote but also gave them a map of how to get there (as well as telling them why it was important to vote).

Do not overlook even the most basic of mechanics – not only where to vote, but how long to allow to vote (if you have not voted for a long time, how do you know if there will be queues?) and what, if any, documentation you need to bring with you to vote. This was important, for example, in a campaign aimed at getting foreign nationals to vote in the 2009 European Parliament elections in the UK – they were entitled to do so but most had no experience of the mechanics of voting in the UK. The same will be true of anyone, wherever they come from, if they have never voted before.

Once you have your answers to the GOTV trio of questions, you can turn your mind to the mechanics.

Target your efforts effectively: turning out more of your opponents' voters than your own will be counter-productive. We witnessed one highly effective Labour Party campaign which won by signing up scores of council tenants to postal votes (postal voters being, on average, twice as likely to vote as everyone else in local council elections). A few months later, the party copied the technique in a nearby town and hugely boosted the majority of the incumbent Liberal

Democrat councillor, who had converted the majority of local council tenants into his personal supporters thanks to years of hard work in the area.

Once you have identified your target voters, though, the approach can be summed up in one word: nag.

List every communications channel you can use – leaflets, letters, phone calls, emails, text messages, tweets, Facebook updates and so on – and then put them together into one integrated timetable for the ten days leading up to polling day.

Not everyone will get every communication of course, but work out how the different channels can supplement each other. The more high tech (emails, social media, text messages) then generally the better the channels are for quick reminders as the close of poll nears. For people with postal votes time the schedule around the dates for delivery of postal ballots and the deadline for their return.

With each message remember to provide the three key pieces of information – why voting will make a difference, how the result will matter and how to actually vote. Do that and more of your supporters will turn out, which in a close contest is the difference between winning and losing.

CHAPTER 88

AT THE COUNT

It's not over 'til it's over.

There was a time when no one but the most hardened political activist was aware of the inner workings of an election count. Indeed, in an age of exit polls and wall-to-wall news coverage it barely seemed necessary to have a count at all. Then along came the 2000 US presidential election and suddenly the world was an expert on hanging chads.

There may never be another election like it: George Bush and Al Gore locked in months of legal wrangling before the result could be officially declared. Yet the point is, elections can be won or lost at the count. Not simply in the formal sense that the count determines the result but in the very practical sense that in close contests the difference between having a good agent and counting observation colleagues and bad ones can make the difference between winning or losing. Both of the authors have witnessed election counts where the agent for a candidate messed up, such as by failing to ask for a recount when they could have, and as a result quite possibly cost their candidate the election.

Impartial staff may do the counting itself, but candidates, agents and their teams have a role a little like lawyers at a public inquiry – they can question and query, and as a result sometimes spot errors or omissions.

The agent therefore needs to be well briefed on the relevant election law before a count, including knowing what decisions they can reasonably question and, if necessary, the appropriate parts of law to quote. They should also make sure they have the name and number of someone to call from the count for a second opinion and further advice in the case of legal emergencies.

The key points to look out for are: have all the ballot boxes come in from all the polling stations, are all the votes counted (do the totals look right compared to how many ballot papers were issued?), is it close enough to ask for a recount, and querying ambiguous ballot papers.

Another top tip from our experience is to ensure you have a fresh and well-briefed team of helpers at the count. Brief them properly because count observers have a crucial job to do. Make sure they are fresh – election day is the longest day of the campaign. If someone works hard from early on election day they may struggle to focus on a count that begins just before midnight and may continue through the night. So, identify your team for the count early and ask them to ensure they are able to cope with a long haul. Get them together before election day and explain to them what their job will be and why it matters.

At election counts in the UK the candidate's legal agent is king. They are the ones who the election officials will turn to with any questions that need an answer from the campaign. So make sure the agent has stayed on the right side of sanity to the end of the campaign. And make sure you support the agent at the count by appointing someone to manage the team of helpers.

The other part of a count is the reaction to the result: dignified or petulant, graceful or sulky? Three-times defeated challenger for the Conservative Party leadership Ken Clarke made losing with grace into a (for him) somewhat unfortunate art form. Graceful defeat served him well, not only earning him popularity with colleagues and the public but also helping smooth the path to his eventual return to the Conservative Party front bench and then the Cabinet.

Win or lose, react with style.

CHAPTER 89

THE ETHICS OF
POLITICAL ARGUMENT

*You're fighting an election, not writing
a Royal Commission report.*

Imagine you are in a courtroom, hearing the prosecution and defence lawyers putting their case in a criminal trial. There is some controversy over the DNA evidence and there has been conflicting evidence from witnesses.

As you hear the prosecution sum up its case, do you expect the lawyer to talk up in detail all the weaknesses in the prosecution case? Of course not. That is what the defence lawyer is there for.

The prosecution lawyer is there to put their case as well as possible. Simply completely ignoring counter-arguments is rarely smart because it leaves too many questions about your case either unanswered or only answered by the other side. But that does not mean a lawyer should dawdle over the weak point in their case, drawing attention to the questionable points and giving criticisms a long hearing. That is not their job.

So, too, in political debate. Your job is to put the case for voting for you. The other candidates put their own cases. The public is the jury who comes up with the verdict.

It is for the jury/voter to weigh up the arguments,

as put to them as convincingly as possible by each side in their own self-interest. It is not for the lawyers/ politicians to offer up not only the reasons for backing them but also the reasons for not doing so.

As with lawyers, there most certainly are some actions that go too far. Faking evidence, browbeating people or bribing the jury/voters are all out. Think of yourself as a lawyer, not a criminal.

Think of yourself too as a lawyer, not an academic writing a Royal Commission report. Your role is not to give a comprehensive summary of all sides of an issue. It is to put your own case as persuasively as you can.

A good academic provides all sides of an argument, weighing up conflicting evidence before presenting their own preferred conclusion. But politics is about the public choosing between candidates – and that means each side putting its own case.

That case can include pointing out the flaws in the other side. If someone has a policy that is flawed or a candidate who is not up to the job, it absolutely is your job to point it out. Unless, of course, you think that someone not being up to the job is not relevant when it comes to deciding who should do the job.

A good political message is a balance. As former Liberal Democrat leader Paddy Ashdown puts it, 'Political messages have to have both a "push" and a "pull" element: that is, your message has to give people a good reason *not* to vote for your opponent as well as a good reason *for* voting for you.'

It can be all too easy for a candidate, campaign or – above all – a group of supporters to get so fired up by the energy of a campaign that in their zeal to do just that they go too far on the push element. So remember to make sure that not only do you have your clear ethical lines, but that you communicate them clearly to everyone on the campaign.

We believe passionately in the value of public institutions and that everyone benefits from the highest standards in public service. We hope you will go well beyond the minimum standards. However, you also have a duty to put your case effectively.

No one ever cleaned up politics by finishing second.

CHAPTER 90

BRINGING IT ALL TOGETHER

Communicating is like cooking.

Given the dreadful diets that most people working intensively on election campaigns end up with, the idea that good campaigning is like good cooking may appear to be a diversion into irony. Bear with us.

Good cooking relies on both good ingredients and a successful cooking process. Really good chefs can cook so well that even mediocre ingredients make for magical dishes, and the finest fresh-cut, hand-picked, organic fruit of the gods turns into an undistinguished mush in the hands of a bad cook.

Success lies in the skilful combination of the right elements into a cohesive whole; so too in political campaigning.

Across the preceding chapters we have set out what our experience tells us is the best recipe for political communication. As with all successful communication, at its core is the need to understand your audience. You need to understand how they prefer to receive information and what information will most effectively engage them.

Voters have more and more channels through which they can receive information. That means that you need to be making use of as many different media as possible in order to maximise your reach. It also means that people can be more and more selective about the information sources they use and the information they take in. Most can choose from scores of TV channels (only a fraction of which will carry current affairs). They can access an almost infinite number of websites and they have an increasingly diverse range of personal networks that they interact with. In every way, people are more mobile. Therefore, your campaign has to talk directly to them about the issues they care about. And it has to do it repeatedly in order to get noticed.

You need to build your own media but you must not neglect the structures that are already there and that can be used to help you: journalists, for example, and your own supporters.

Once you have identified and clarified your message you will need to use it to persuade people to vote for you – you do not need to persuade everyone; if you try to do that you will almost certainly fail, if not as a candidate then as a representative. The persuasion will involve opening people's minds to the possibility of voting for you, convincing them that they should vote for you and then motivating them to get down to the polling station to place that cross on the ballot paper. All of these steps can be made easier using the campaigning tips that are in this book. But none of those techniques will work effectively if the raw material is not right. Beautifully cooked rotten fish gives you food poisoning, not pleasure.

From reading this book, you will end up with many new ideas and schemes to add to your existing knowledge and intention. You now need to blend them together into a coherent plan, one that both prioritises and makes the whole more than the sum of the parts. That is partly why we dedicated so many sections at the start of the book to getting your message right. That is important in itself, but also a good, clear message provides the right basis for people working on different parts of the campaign to work together in a complementary, rather than contradictory way, even if they are not talking to each other all the time.

A good organisational plan to go with the clear message further helps. In addition, you need to be sure that there is at least one person in charge with an overview of the different elements of your campaign, so they can spot potential contradictions and exploit possibilities for complementary action.

PART 5

LEADERSHIP

Nelson Mandela said leadership was about putting others in front when you celebrate victory and putting yourself in front when you face danger. This book examines the processes and the human skills you need to marshal in order to win. Few elements are as difficult to define as what makes a good leader. You may not face dangers and victories on the same scale as Nelson Mandela but generosity and bravery are skills anyone can master. Leadership is a vital part of a successful campaign.

CHAPTER 91

GET YOUR LIFE OUTSIDE POLITICS SORTED

All tip and no iceberg.
Paul Keating on Peter Costello

The sense that Australian Liberal politician Peter Costello was all superficial political communication and no substance triggered Labor man and insulter extraordinaire Paul Keating's jibe that Costello was 'all tip and no iceberg'.

Having a hinterland can help to make the person a better politician. In the UK former Labour Party leader John Smith once spoke of how he only knew about the latest computer games because of his children – they gave him a perspective on life that is otherwise too easy to lose inside a political hothouse atmosphere.

The years since have made his comment all the more apposite, for the question of what taxes and regulations should govern the computer games industry have regularly come up in Britain. Having a passing understanding of those things, which so many people spend so many hours playing, is not only necessary to retain touch with the outside world for a politician, it is also necessary to be able to make political decisions well.

More importantly, though, having a hinterland helps to make the politician a better person. Whether it is a hobby, an interest or just a way of relaxing outside of politics helps many a politician keep sane. Given the importance of making high-pressure decisions during a campaign or once in office and making them well, sanity is not to be under-rated. (Think of some politicians and you will also realise sanity is also not to be taken for granted.)

The public, too, often warms to politicians who have a human (though not too human) side to them. British Conservative Ken Clarke's love of jazz and Ken Livingstone's fondness for newts have both helped their political appeal. Not too emotional, not too upper class, not too geeky.

Not that we are suggesting a candidate needs to create a hobby to fit their electoral profile. In the UK there are already too many politicians who claim a life-long affinity to a football team when it is fairly obvious that they had never thought of the game until an election came along. Our point is much more that a genuine outside interest will keep you grounded (and if it does not look too eccentric to voters then that is a bonus!).

Keeping some of that non-political interest going can be tough, which is even more reason to explicitly plan for it.

Some steps are almost trivial, such as making sure that before a campaign you stock up with birthday cards and presents ready to use, and you switch as many bills as possible to automatic payment. Face the pressure of an election campaign with an irate relative whose birthday you ignored and a utilities company chasing for an unpaid bill and you quickly realise the benefits of getting some of the basics organised in advance.

Taking the time in advance to talk to family and friends, to spend a little extra time with them and to warn them what to expect, is what many wise politicians also do. They are, after all, yours to love or to lose for life, far longer than even the lengthiest campaign or term of office.

Politics and modern government is a complex business. We are not dewy-eyed sentimentalists who long for an age of gentlemen politicians who tend to the nation in between tending to their country estate.

Government needs more attention, more time and more professionalism than the old part-time amateurs could provide. But anyone who ends up being 100 per cent politician all the time will not be a good politician. The best politicians are still human beings, remembering to care about those outside politics and remembering not to be totally consumed by it.

CHAPTER 92

EXCELLENCE

*We are what we repeatedly do; excellence is not
an act but a habit.* Nicomachean Ethics

Excellence is not like electricity. It is not something you can simply turn on when required and expect to start flowing. Rather it is a habit, something you acquire by regular practice until it becomes second nature and instinctive. The training and experience that comes with repetition is what excellence needs.

Repetition makes excellent behaviour a habit, bringing two crucial advantages for the over-worked political campaigner. First, the better your habits and the higher the standards they reach, the better protected you are against the inevitable slippage as exhaustion, pressure and a shortage of time all combine to waylay even the best of campaigners. If you are normally excellent and circumstances occasionally bring you down a notch to good, that is fine; if you are normally mediocre, however, they will reduce you to poor and that is anything but fine.

That is not the only advantage excellence brings. As excellence becomes a habit in one area, you can spend time thinking and practising on the next. Those who settle for mediocre not only slip to poor in the pressures of an election but they also fail to expand their skills if they are always battling just to be mediocre. If you want an outstanding election result you need to run an outstanding campaign.

Moreover, you can never quite be sure what moment of detail will turn out to be crucial. At a computer, a failure to check may not mess up one email but hundreds of thousands of target letters, or a sloppy policy promise may not be a quickly forgotten comment to a supporter but something turned into headline news by the journalist standing just behind. Unless you seek for excellence, sloppiness will not only infect the campaign, it will catch you out both when you think matters are trivial and also when they are vital.

As President Bill Clinton's campaign manager James Carville put it, 'You'll find a hundred people in a campaign headquarters who, among them, have a thousand different theories. But you'll only find a handful who actually have an idea *and* the ability to implement it.'

Some people treat political success like trying to get rich by buying a lottery ticket each week. You can be lazy, indolent and not really try to get rich for most of the week, but buy the lottery ticket and who knows? Perhaps you will be the lucky one and get rich without having tried.

If you have been putting in the hard work to try to get rich and you see someone pull off a lottery win, it can be annoying, to say the least. But thinking that is the right strategy for you is like saying, 'Well, I don't really want this so I don't mind having almost no chance of pulling it off.'

If you really want it, you need to make better odds for yourself.

So, too, with politics. The occasional unlikely combination of circumstances does propel the mediocre into office, but if you really want office you need to excel. Not when the election itself comes round, not next month, but from today onwards.

CHAPTER 93

YOU'RE NOT PERFECT

I've failed over and over and over again in my life.
And that is why I succeed. Michael Jordan

Persuaded by our previous section that you need to make a habit of excellence, how do you set about it? With humility and with understanding that you are not perfect. If you cannot learn and improve, you are not listening.

However, learning is not simply about listening to the wisdom and experience of others; it is also about trying – and therefore inevitably about failing.

You tend to notice people once they have become excellent, so it is easy to think they were always excellent, overlooking the time and work it took to become that way.

If you never make a mistake, you have not been trying to learn. But if you carry on making the same mistake again and again, you are simply stuck learning the same lesson again and again. Success comes from making new and different mistakes, learning new and different lessons each time. Do not worry, though – you can also learn from when things go right!

In fact, the Israeli Defence Force put this to the test with two companies of soldiers training in navigation skills. One company had four days of exercises and after each carried out a review looking at what lessons they could learn from things that went wrong. The second company did the same exercises over four days, but its reviews both looked at what went wrong and also learned lessons from what went right.

These companies then went through another two days of navigation exercises two months later. They had both improved substantially, but it was the second company – the one that had reviewed success as well as failure – that had improved the most.

That is particularly important in politics, which can at times be unforgiving, with the unsuccessful not getting a chance to try again. Some political cultures are far more forgiving of failure than others, most notably Australia's. Despite the super-heated acerbic rhetoric that is the norm in Australian politics, resigning a leadership position after a humiliating defeat is very often but an interim pause in a political career rather than the end of it.

Wider academic research backs up the point: humans learn more from failure than from success, but learn best when learning from failure and success.

Learning of any sort is, in our experience, too rarely invested in when it comes to politics. We have talked earlier about the importance of building teams and of ensuring that square pegs are found square holes to fit into in the campaign structure. But there should be more to it than that. We believe that you should be developing people through the campaign, too. You should build training plans into your wider campaign plan (and budget).

The immediate advantage of investing in training is clear: if you train people to perform tasks well then your campaign will run better. The longer-term advantage is that they will be more committed to you and your cause. If you broaden the skills that people in your campaign have then you are broadening the number of people who can be involved in the key tasks, increasing capacity and building in durability.

But remember that that learning is not just for others; it is also for you.

CHAPTER 94

TRAIN YOURSELF
AND TRAIN OTHERS

That which is good is never finished. Tanzanian proverb

In Chapter 93 we explained why we think training is important. However, in the heat of an election campaign, how do you do it in practice?

Read this book, believe everything we say, implement everything we recommend – job done? Alas no. Not only is there the risk your opponent might also have purchased this book (we recommend you minimise this risk by regularly visiting your local bookshops and buying up all the stock, just in case), but much of the skill is in the implementation – you need to do it and do it well. That means there is always more to learn and more to get better at, even leaving aside how changes in politics, society and technology mean that one year's perfect campaign is another year's failure.

You should therefore think of learning and training as a continuous process, both for yourself and, crucially, for your team members.

You will find some people who think they know it all, and finding ways of gracefully putting them right is necessary. This can lead to difficult conversations but those are often the conversations that most need to be had. Try to set out how the task fits into the campaign plan and how you have taken advice from experts. Support your case with facts but make sure the evidence is on your side. One author was floored when persuading a seasoned helper to make one last 'get out the vote' effort on election day. He tried the line 'Have you ever known anyone vote against us just because we knocked on their door to remind them to vote?', which elicited an unchallengeable 'Yes' from the reluctant helper.

One example of the importance of learning is delivering leaflets. There is a lot people can learn: the quickest way to plan a route, ensuring leaflets are pushed through letterboxes in case the resident is away from home, knowing if there is likely to be an extra apartment door round the side or back of a building, the ability to collect, record and report data en route. Yet many people will ridicule the idea that they can learn more about how to deliver leaflets, for it is just about stuffing something through the letter-boxes, isn't it?

Equally, even with the simplest task new helpers might need guidance. Do you deliver a leaflet to a door that has a sign requesting no junk mail? Do you deliver it to the home that is displaying your opponent's poster? Why are there some leaflets left over at the end of the round? Why did you run out before the end of the round? Small things like this can worry and even deter helpers. A small amount of time invested in introducing new helpers to each task will be rewarded with greater efficiency – and hopefully more willing helpers.

With a little diplomacy you can open up people's minds. Try, for example, giving a deliverer a set of addressed items to deliver, which means as they go door to door they discover for themselves that they do not know where all the letterboxes are. Get them to submit ideas to help train new people on how to find hard-to-locate addresses and they will end up learning for themselves too.

We have deliberately chosen to focus on what seems to be the simplest of tasks to help us stress again how important training is, but it runs through the tasks that make up a campaign. Plan sessions to train groups of new volunteers. Get experienced team members to record their expertise so that you build a bank of 'institutional knowledge' that can be shared with others. Identify mentors and pair them up with those who need mentoring. Open up internal communication – encourage a culture of sharing. Make contact with other campaigns and send teams to learn from them (they do not have to be election campaigns). Look around for other sources of training not directly aimed at political campaigns.

Build training and development into your campaign plan and you will be rewarded by a more effective team that develops as it grows.

CHAPTER 95

EVERYTHING IS IMPOSSIBLE IF YOU DON'T TRY

Failure is not falling down but refusing to get up.
Chinese proverb

Failure is remarkably popular with successful people. It is not that they like to fail or that they fail frequently, but failure has often been a large part of what made them successful. It is no coincidence that our language abounds with quotes, proverbs and clichés about how failure and practice can be turned into success. The general message is a simple one – do not be put off by failure but learn from your mistakes.

That willingness to try is all the more important because in politics apparently insurmountable odds often turn out different. Landslide victories get followed by defeats, most popular politicians slip to the least popular end of the league table and impregnable majorities disappear at the next election.

Since the nineteenth century, parliamentary reference work Dods has regularly produced profiles of parliamentary constituencies. Its 2004 profile of Hornsey & Wood Green, in north London, described the then Labour MP's majority as 'probably impregnable'. A year later she was defeated in a campaign which Mark managed.

The factors behind why the apparently impossible

in elections can turn out to be very possible are many, including the increasing volatility of the electorate as fewer people have one party they always vote for through their whole life, and the increasing sophistication of campaign techniques and technologies that offer up more ways of persuading people to change their minds. In the mix is the long-standing habit of some politicians resting on their laurels once elected, making that apparently large majority far more brittle than it may appear if someone puts it to the test. It is easy to sit back when you face challenges from candidates who are not very good or only half-try, or try very hard but only for a few weeks. When faced with a good candidate who tries hard over a long period, a majority can become very vulnerable.

Following every bit of advice in this book will not guarantee you success. Based on our experience we believe it will increase your chances but good fortune and the behaviour of your opponents are bound to play a role, too.

Winning campaigns often occur when the candidate faces unpopular opponents. But not, by any means, always. To increase your chances of winning you probably need to make three profound choices. First, that it is what you really (really) want to do with your life. Second, that you are prepared to lose (sometimes more than once) on the way to winning. Third, that you are not just prepared to learn from those defeats but that you will actively seek out the learning.

In the United States, Bill Clinton has most embodied these characteristics. No doubt myth has woven with truth to create the story we know now, but merely the fact that Clinton built his image on early failings is testament to his abilities. Elected a state governor at the age of thirty he was thrown out of office within two years. He blew his keynote speech at a Democrat Convention but re-learned the skills of oratory and restored his credibility as a candidate. And then there were the 'difficulties' over his personal life and his early policy failures from which he came back to win election and re-election as President.

Clinton never gave up. He used his mistakes to develop and used his experiences to craft a story about himself that helped him further. Not trying at all guarantees not only failure but no lessons to learn from. Trying and failing opens up a world of opportunities.

CHAPTER 96

TIME MANAGEMENT

The less one has to do, the less time one finds to do it in.
Lord Chesterfield

One sure way of wasting time is to sit at a computer, fire up an internet search engine and look for advice on time management. The hours can slip by one after another as you then drown in the myriad of different tips and advice available, though they all always say that part of the answer to better time management is to spend more time reading their advice or buying their book or doing their training. None warns against spending too much time on their advice...

However, there are some common themes and very sensible tips in this huge field.

First, prioritise. Sounds obvious, but knowing what you need to do first is central to efficient use of time. This can be harder than it sounds, as you need to balance urgency and importance – simply always doing what is immediately pressing may mean more important, less time-sensitive tasks are never done. You also need to remember to balance the items where there is a direct and indirect impact on others, especially ones where the 'cost' is that of volunteer time being wasted.

Second, avoid prevarication. For many people, this

is the hardest part. Having good intentions and good plans is not enough if you then start stalling when something you do not really like doing comes to the head of the list. The classic solution to this is to break tasks down into small chunks both so that you are never put off by feeling something is too big to start just now and so it seems less unpleasant to do. However, it still leaves the problem that the next thing to do might be one you just do not want to do. We like the advice given by Stever Robbins in *Get It Done Guy's 9 Steps to Work Less and Do More*: breaking tasks down not into small chunks but into slices of time. Saying 'I'll spend ten minutes doing this and then stop regardless of where I have got to' is much easier as you know all you need do is spend ten minutes.

Third, cut out inefficient use of time. What can you make more efficient, particularly with a little invest-ment of time up front – such as finding out how to do mail-merge letters properly on your computer? Keep a little diary over a few days to see what really eats up your time – and learn from that.

Fourth, have a system. All three of the above steps are much easier if you have a system. At this point you can waste a large amount of time by trying to decide what system to use, for there are nearly as many time-management systems as there are taxi drivers who think they are smarter than every politician. As with many things in life, picking the perfect system does not really matter; a half-decent, well-imple-mented system starting soon counts for more than a perfect system that never quite gets started.

Often the most effective way of learning how to manage time is to ask other people if they have seen you wasting it. A particularly effective leader that

Ed worked for says that one of the most important conversations he ever had was when his best friend sat him down and told him how much he annoyed colleagues by always being late for meetings. Since then he appreciated how being late gave the impression that he did not value their time and now he organises his time so he is (almost) never late for appointments. He wins respect as a result and gets through meetings more efficiently too!

The classic mistake is to spend too much time being busy and not enough time being organised. Do not make it.

CHAPTER 97

ADAPT OR DIE

*Victory awaits him who has everything in order –
luck, people call it.* Roald Amundsen

In Britain, Amundsen is known as the faintly obscure Norwegian who got to the South Pole ahead of Scott of the Antarctic. While Scott and his team are immortalised for their heroic deaths, Amundsen is the person relegated to the footnotes – getting there first and living not being enough to grab the limelight.

Even allowing for the natural instinct to be more interested in the achievements of people from your own country, there is something not wholly flattering about the British veneration of someone who failed while the man who triumphed is usually relegated to being that Norwegian chap whose first name you cannot spell.

But there is a much wider lesson about Roald Amundsen: he learned how to adapt in order to survive in polar regions while Scott was trying and failing to use brute force.

In 1903, Amundsen and his team became the first to travel the North West Passage from the Atlantic to the Pacific – succeeding where people had failed over the previous centuries. On the way, he spent much time learning from natives their survival skills

296

for a hostile environment. He learned to use relatively light animal skins for warmth instead of the very heavy European-style coats. Staying warm without being burdened down with weight was an important edge. He also learned to use light sledges pulled by dogs rather than the more traditional combination of heavy sledges and ponies. This was smart adaptation to the circumstances rather than ponderous use of heavy equipment not really suited for the environment.

Those lessons served Amundsen well on his trip to the South Pole, in contrast to Scott's reliance on heavy equipment not well suited to the conditions. Amundsen himself put his success down to the prior learning and the resulting preparation.

The lesson for candidates? Learn and adapt. There will be those who you can learn from (as Amundsen learned from the natives in the Arctic), there will be ways you can adapt nimbly to your environment, be it physical or virtual.

Have the humility to learn from those who have won before. Seek them out and ask them. One of your authors vividly recalls an evening spent in a new candidate's kitchen soaking up the experience of an older candidate who was in the process of building a winning team in his own town. Not everything that was discussed entered the campaign plan but it helped to shape it. Both candidates went on to win.

Borrow knowledge from other fields. Look at how successful organisations organise; look at how successful campaigners campaign. Do not limit yourself to the world of political elections: figure out how you can apply knowledge and experience that may not be an obvious fit at first glance.

Learn, adapt – and succeed.

CHAPTER 98

BE TRANSPARENT, ETHICAL AND ACCOUNTABLE

*The hardest thing about any political campaign is how
to win without proving that you are unworthy
of winning.* Adlai Stevenson

Every year the public relations firm Edelman publishes what it calls a global 'Trust Monitor'. As the name suggests it measures trust in key institutions. It is deliberately selective – it only polls what you might call the 'chattering classes'. But it does not make great reading for politicians. In the UK, trust in government bobbles around the 40 per cent mark, similar to the US, India and Italy. The only institution consistently less trusted around the world is the media.

MORI's regular polling on the British public's trust of different politicians tells a story that is little better. In some years, politicians do not finish bottom of the league table; but that is only because they just pip journalists.

Despite those low scores (or maybe because of them), in politics as in business, trust is an increasingly important asset, especially as traditional loyalties to particular parties are weakening, meaning fewer and fewer candidates can rely on tribal loyalty to see them past the winning post.

You should always behave ethically but that is not the same as making your ethical stance a centrepiece of your campaign. You can run as the modern-day Mr Smith coming to clean up town. Or you can run on other issues and simply ensure that your ethical judgements match up to your other promises. That leaves you, the aspiring candidate, with an important choice. Where on the trust-o-meter scale of political ethics, from Nixon to Gandhi, do you want to be and where will the public think you are?

The first step is to ensure you comply with the rules. Make sure you understand the rules for campaign spending and disclosure. Make sure you understand the rules governing what you can and cannot say about your campaign and your opponents. For a politician, in this area, ignorance will most certainly provide no defence.

Ensure that you have a structure in place to manage these issues. The appropriate structure will depend on the scale of your campaign but do not do it all yourself. Avoid giving the responsibility entirely to one other person, too. Even if you trust them implicitly, a single mistake can lead to severe consequences.

The next step is to decide how far ethics will define your campaign. Running against 'Washington insiders' has a long-established track record in the US. That hints at a different way of doing politics, one that suggests the incumbents have lost their connection with voters' values. There are fewer successful examples in the UK but the MPs' expenses scandal of 2009 has changed the zeitgeist. It has raised the profile of ethics on the campaign trail, and candidates and incumbents are increasingly making disclosure a prominent part of their message.

If you choose to make ethics a centrepiece of your campaign, make sure you live by the rule. Reputation can be squandered in an instant – communication and consistency is vital. Recall the 'Back to Basics' campaign as an example. In the mid-1990s the Conservative government in the UK was struggling to restore its reputation after a key part of its economic agenda fell apart. The Prime Minister launched a 'Back to Basics' campaign that promoted traditional values. Within weeks the campaign – and the government – was ruined by a series of sex and financial scandals involving ministers. In the end, the campaign had made the situation worse because it failed to reflect the actual behaviour of government ministers.

Therefore, the final step is to consider how ethics shapes your communication strategy. Do you make a virtue of running an ethical campaign that goes beyond basic disclosure and compliance with the law? Do you make institutional changes a key campaign pledge?

If you do, you can offer up extra transparency – such as prompt listing of donors on your website and fuller disclosure of expense claims than the rules require. However, you also offer yourself up to be held to a higher standard by the public and the media – both of whom love berating hypocrisy.

Firmly avoiding putting yourself on a pedestal does not remove the need to ensure you follow the rules and do not make yourself the victim of the sort of scandal that has made you eagerly read the newspaper reports on others in the past.

CHAPTER 99

WHAT IF YOU LOSE?

There is no comparison between that which is lost by not succeeding and that lost by not trying. Francis Bacon

Often the most elegant and dignified speech a candidate makes during a campaign is their concession speech, admitting they have lost. Losing with dignity is better than losing in a sulk, but it is still losing. So there should be two priorities for the losing candidate: to wrap up matters in a respectful and dignified way and to start, however slowly, the process of understanding what needs to be different to win next time, whether it is for them personally or a successor.

What you should not do is what former MP Lembit Öpik did on losing the selection to be a candidate for London mayor. He compared his defeat in that contest to Nelson Mandela's decades in jail. Not surprisingly, no one else thought losing a contest to be a candidate was comparable to decades in jail.

Humility not hubris is the right reaction to defeat – as Michael Portillo demonstrated so well following his shock defeat as an MP in the 1997 general election. Despite the result becoming one of the classic TV clips of the election, his grace in defeat meant its frequent replaying served to bolster his reputation rather than denigrate it by reminding everyone he was a failure.

Helpers and supporters need thanking – with extra time and attention given to those who helped the most. Be generous with the hand-written thank-you notes, the tokens of appreciation and the time for personal conversations.

Losing an election can be a little bit like a family bereavement. Do not forget that other members of the family – your campaign team – will feel the loss almost as acutely as you. Invest time in finding out what they got from the campaign and what they want to take from it (is there a future candidate among them?). Then work out how you can help them to achieve that. And, if you can, keep supporting them.

Pay attention to the party organisation that backed your campaign. Can the centre learn things from your campaign? Can you support them with your knowledge and time in other ways? Do you need to attend to gaps that have appeared in the local organisation's infrastructure (its bank balance, for example!)?

A common theme through this book has been the importance of data, so of course wrapping up the data records matters, making sure the last pieces of information during the frenzy up until the close of polling are all tidied up and stored away for future use.

There is always various legal paperwork that needs sorting after an election. It is not only winning candidates who need to follow the law.

Do not lose sight of your obligations to voters. Someone who comes to you with an urgent housing problem the day before the election deserves to have that problem addressed whatever the result of the election. Even if it is to brief your victorious opponent, make sure you have a plan for dealing with outstanding issues.

And then it is time to start learning the lessons. With a painful defeat it may be wise to take time and start learning the lessons slowly, but learn them everyone should. An effective debrief and sharing of views will not only help learn the lessons for the future, it will also help people draw a line under defeat and be ready to work together harmoniously and hard for the next contest. Learning the lessons from defeat is not optional – unless you want to carry on losing.

But remember, many of the most successful candidates have lost more than once and in politics, as in life, it is far better to try, fail and try again than never to try in the first place.

CHAPTER 100

WHAT IF YOU WIN?

Whoever is winning at the moment will always seem to be invincible. George Orwell

Nearly everything that applies to losing (see Chapter 99) applies to winning, too – but all the more so. If you win, you have the privilege and burden of taking up office. You will have many tasks to perform but remember that one of them is to prepare for your next campaign. That means keeping a team of helpers is all the more important. Start by thanking them. And remember to ask them to stay involved: you need to start building your next campaign team the day after the election is over.

The potential political fallout if it turns out you did not follow all the legal rules is also all the greater if you win, so again making sure that the paperwork is properly sorted out and the necessary official declarations made is important.

When you win there may appear to be less need to debrief and analyse the result than if you lose, but just as losing is a great teacher so too can be winning – if you remember to learn the lessons. George Orwell had it right when he warned against the hubris that can come with winning and the assumption that just because you won last time you will always win in future. It does not mean that. It means you won last time, no more and no less. The wise winning candidate remembers humility and the need to work out why they won (and no, it was not because you were just so brilliant that you deserved to win) so they have a head start on working out what to do next time.

Before next time there is the little matter of doing the job to which you have been elected. Campaigning and communicating do not – or rather should not – stop on taking up office. Do not disappear into an anonymous bunker. Continue to let the public know what you are up to, solicit their views and treat politics as a two-way conversation just as you did campaigning. Hit the ground running: days lost at the beginning can leave you with the permanent feeling that you are running to catch up. Ideally, find someone you trust to start planning your transition to office well *before* you know the result of the election. Having someone take the strain on finding office space, planning staff recruitment and preparing how you will deal with correspondence can save you a mountain of stress. It can help you do a better job because voters who need you to deal with an issue do not need to wait weeks while you sort out your office and then catch up on the backlog.

Live by the promises you made as a candidate. Of course, we are cynical enough to recognise that not doing so will damage your chances of getting re-elected. However, there is a good reason why the two things are linked: when they vote for you, people place their trust in you. Many will have gone further. They will have talked to their friends and maybe even persuaded some of them to vote for you. Some will have displayed a poster for you. Some will have delivered leaflets or knocked on doors for you. A handful will have put their normal lives on hold to spend days (and nights) helping your campaign.

They deserve to know that you have been honest with yourself and with them during the campaign and that you will stay that way once you are elected.

CHAPTER 101

HOW TO USE THIS BOOK

Knowing is not enough; we must apply. Willing is not enough; we must do. Johann Wolfgang von Goethe

Goethe had a point. Knowing what you need to do to win is easy. Wanting to win is not that much harder. But actually doing it – that is essential. Or, as Margaret Thatcher put it, 'What is success? I think it is a mixture of having a flair for the thing that you are doing; knowing that it is not enough, that you have got to have hard work and a certain sense of purpose.'

By now you are bursting with knowledge from this book (or have cheated and skipped straight to the end, hoping you will find an easy, miracle formula revealed there; sorry to disappoint). Turning that knowledge into action is what will make the difference between you thinking 'Good book, nice authors' (which we're quite happy for you to think, by the way) and celebrating victory in a future campaign.

We deliberately structured the book around easy-to-digest short sections so that in future you can dip in and out of the book as needed. Whatever the next big campaigning challenge coming up, take a flick through the book and look at the sections that are most applicable.

Many of the points in the book will most apply to what other people working on your campaign get up to. Knowing what they should be doing is the first step to good management and delegation – as long as it leads to just that and not control-freakery micro-management.

We would also suggest that, aside from keeping the book to hand for future occasions, you sit down now and list the five chapters you thought you learned the most from. Make it a habit to check back and think about them every two or three weeks for the next three months. By then, those five sections should be second nature to you. So move on to the next group of five. And so on until you can look back on the book and think, 'Money well spent. When are the authors writing another?'

Reading a book with good intentions is easy. The hard work starts now. Good luck.